from
Grandpa,   **The Real Arsenal Story**

for the Critchley
family after a
great boys' day
out!

October 2015.

# The
# Real Arsenal
# Story

## In the days of *Gog*

# Alan Roper

Wherry Publishing

First published in the United Kingdom 2004 by
Wherry Publishing
51 Longdells Hills
Costessey
Norwich NR5 0PD

A CIP catalogue record for this book is available from the British Library.

ISBN: 0–9546259–0–0

Designed and edited by Curran Publishing Services, Norwich
Printed and bound in the United Kingdom by
Antony Rowe Ltd, Chippenham and Eastbourne

# Contents

# Illustrations

# Match Reports

## Chapter 2

## Chapter 3

## Chapter 4

## Chapter 5

# Acknowledgements

I would like to thank all the people who have assisted me in making this book possible:

My wife Delia
My eldest son Mark and my niece Elizabeth
Susan Curran and her team
Bob Beardsley Colmer
Bill Charteris
John Gooding (Christmas)
Joan Ostrom (Christmas)
Mrs R H Wyatt (Danskin)
Neville Danskin
Roy Horsington
Lionel Humble (sadly deceased)
Mike Crossman (Julian)
Mrs D W Parr
Alastair Sutherland
Janice O'Brien
Lynne Gardiner
Graham Caldwell
Greenwich Local History Library
Coventry Library Archives
Community Librarian (Heritage) East Ayrshire

I apologise to anyone I have inadvertently missed out.

### Further reading:

Fred Ollier, *Arsenal: A Complete Record*, Breedon Books (1995).
Martin Tyler and Phil Soar, *The Official Illustrated History of Arsenal, 1886–2003*, Hamlyn (2003).

# Preface

The Royal Arsenal Football Club was founded by David Danskin and other Woolwich Arsenal armaments workers in 1886. Due to lack of funding it went into liquidation in 1910. The assets were subsequently acquired by Sir Henry Norris MP and his business associates. They later moved the club to north London and changed the name to Arsenal FC.

This book is about the personal lives and times of these early footballers, and is dedicated to their memory.

# Introduction

Nottingham was thriving due to the increased demand for lace curtains. This was one of the areas where organized football matches originated. Two of the early teams were Notts County and Nottingham Forest. Forest grew out of a club that played an early form of hockey.

In the early 1860s if you had watched either of these clubs play football you would not have understood the game they were playing. To score a goal you kicked the ball between an opponent's inner posts, which were four yards apart. On either side of the posts were rouge flags. If the ball touched down between one of the posts and the rouge flag, a point was scored. There were no referees, and the team captains controlled the games. The number of players to each team was often decided on the day of the match. It was not uncommon to play 17 or 18 players per side.

One of the problems for schools and colleges was the difficulty in playing matches against each other, as each college had its own set of rules. In 1846 there was an early failed attempt by Cambridge to formulate a general set of rules. A second more successful attempt was made in 1862, when many public schools adopted the ten rules set out in *The Simplest Game*, published by J C Thring. This was probably more akin to the 'open game', explained in more detail in the Appendix.

The Football Association rules, which were produced in 1863, were based on the Cambridge rules, and encompassed 14 points including the size of the pitch and the banning of tripping and hacking. Although these rules were used from that date it must be appreciated that at this time many of the teams, even those who were members of the FA, still played to their own adaptation of the rules. For instance, in one story Charles Alcock, later Secretary of the FA, who was tired of Arthur Kinnaird (later Lord Kinnaird) hacking his shins, said, 'Are we playing hacking, Arthur?' Kinnaird replied, 'Oh yes, let's have hacking.' 'It's all right as long as I know', said Alcock, and the pleasant game proceeded.

As soon as the new rules were produced, a major dispute arose in the main over hacking, which led to the breakaway of the Blackheath FC and others. These clubs, eight years later in 1871, were to become founders of the Rugby Union. In time of course the Union also banned hacking. See details of the 'close game' and the laws of Rugby Union (see Appendix).

In 1878 the Lancashire Football Association was formed. The original teams included Blackburn Rovers, Bolton Wanderers, Darwen, Eagley and Turton. Interestingly, Turton published its rules in 1873 (see Appendix). These rules were similar to the 'open game'.

In 1878 Eagley played Darwen in the second round of the FA Cup, and one presumes the prevailing FA Cup rules were used. The Old Etonians won the cup that year.

An interesting but long-winded article about football appeared in *The Times* in November 1880. Some of the more relevant extracts are:

> *Not fifteen years back, few men played football after they left school. The reason was that there was no uniform code of rules, which should regulate the play of clubs. Every school even had its own rules, often connected with the shape or the peculiarities of the playground. Eton, Harrow, Winchester, and a few other schools still cling to distinct types of game endeared by long association. It was only lately that Rugby School abandoned the 'hacking' and 'tripping' which made football dreaded by anxious mothers, and which marked the distaste of the schoolboys for what was new-fangled and humane,*

> *That for every football club and for every player that could be found 15 years ago, there may now be found a hundred.*

> *Many of the strongest clubs about London are composed of 'old boys' from the public schools. The Old Etonians and the Old Harrovians abandon the old school rules and adopt those of the Association. The habits of school days save them from the trouble experienced by other clubs of learning 'to play together'. The Clapham Rovers are, however, the champions for the time being, as the holders of the Association Cup. Among other redoubtable Association Clubs are the Wanderers and the Royal Engineers in the south, Nottingham Forest and Sheffield in the Midlands, Darwen and Blackburn Rovers in Lancashire, and the Vale of Leven and Queen's Park in Scotland. The*

*players of the Rugby Union game are probably twice as numerous as those of the Association. The most powerful suburban clubs are Richmond and Blackheath, the last named of which is probably more than a match for any club or any town in England or Scotland.*

*The ball is shot under the tape or over the bar, and the call of time immediately afterwards proclaims the game at an end; the players of the two teams fraternise; a parching thirst is assuaged with refreshing draughts; to the cold bath succeeds the glow and exhilaration which invariably follow tremendous exercise. If the play is crowned with festivities in the evening in no other circumstances could festivity be so innocuous. In any case the energy, pent up by perhaps a week's sedentary employment has had its outlet.*

What really gripped the imagination of the public was the introduction of the FA Challenge Cup in 1871–2; the first final was between the Wanderers and the Royal Engineers with an attendance of approximately 2,000. The admittance charge was one shilling (five pence in present-day money).

The Royal Engineers were made favourites at 7–4 on. The Engineers were unfortunate in that Lieutenant Cresswell broke a collarbone within 10 minutes of the start. He bravely played to the end. The Wanderers' star player was the Reverend R Vidal who was known for his exceptional dribbling ability. He broke clear and passed to M Betts who duly scored the only goal of the game.

The Wanderers' captain was Charles Alcock, mentioned above, so it was fitting that he should be the first person to be presented with the FA Cup.

The captain of the losing side was another exceptional person, Sir Francis Marindin (President of the FA 1874–90), who was of Huguenot descent. (The Huguenots were French Protestant refugees who settled in England during the seventeenth and eighteeenth centuries.) Marindin was educated at Eton and went to work at the Woolwich Arsenal. He was so successful there that he was awarded a commission in the Royal Engineers. In those days teams normally relied on individuals who could dribble long distances on the field. Major Marindin, as he was later known, was one of the first soccer tacticians. The Sappers coached by him concentrated on teamwork.

During that period against top-class opposition, they played 86 matches, losing only three, with a goal scoring record of 244 and only conceding 21.

Although he was of French descent, Marindin was proud to be an English subject. He refereed a cup semi-final between Preston North End and West Bromwich Albion in 1887. After the match he went into the dressing room of the successful Albion side and asked them if they were all Englishmen. 'Yes', was the unanimous reply. The Major said, 'I have very much pleasure in presenting you with the ball. You played a very good game and I hope you will win the cup.' In fact Aston Villa were the winners in that year by 2–0. Villa's first goal was hotly disputed but both umpires ruled it a goal. (The referee only arbitrated if the umpires disagreed. His main function was to act as timekeeper, and he was positioned off the playing field.)

The Engineers were again runners up in 1874. They finally won the cup in 1875, beating the Old Etonians 2–0 after a replay. Sadly the Major was no longer playing. He was in time to influence first Nottingham Forest and then Arsenal in their tactical play. Major Marindin officiated in eight finals.

Another notable early football player was the previously mentioned Lord Arthur Fitzgerald Kinnaird (the eleventh Baron) (1847–1923), a banker partner in Barclay Ransom & Co and President of FA from 1890 to 1923. He was the son of the Hon. Arthur Fitzgerald Kinnaird MP and the Hon. Mrs Mary Jane Kinnaird, and was no doubt spoilt as a child, being the only boy and having six sisters. Two interesting stories were told about him. In the first, Lord Kinnaird's mother was talking to Major Marindin. She regretted that Arthur was always playing football and was sure one day he would return home with a broken leg. 'Pray do not be alarmed', said the Major, 'for if anybody's leg is broken it will not be Arthur's'.

The second story concerns Tom Maley, who played for a Scottish eleven against a team that included Kinnaird. Maley was getting very upset at the play he was receiving from Kinnaird, and said, 'If you do that again, my man, I'll pull your whiskers for ye!' A member of Tom's team rushed up and said to Tom, 'Do ye no ken that's the Honourable Arthur Kinnaird?' He answered, 'I dinna care who he is, if he does that again I'll pull his whiskers.' (Willie Maley and his brother Tom were in the Celtic team that later won the Scottish Cup in 1892. Willie was to serve the Celtic Club as both an administrator and manager for 50 years).

Lord Kinnaird was to write that some of the roughest games he played in had not been with northern or professional teams but in matches with clubs representing public schools and universities. An example was H A Goodhart of the Old Etonians, a very big and heavy man who simply ran over anyone who came in his way.

In 1866 Kinnaird played in a representative match for London against Sheffield. The London side won by two goals and four touch-downs to nothing.

For all his rough play, Kinnaird was an outstanding player for over 30 years, in which time he must have played under a series of vastly different rules. Even in the period where he played in the Cup Finals there were major changes:

1871    The goalkeeper was allowed to use his hands. Referees were first used to resolve disputes between the umpires in the later rounds of the FA Cup.

1873    Corner kicks first officially adopted.

1875    Cross-bars were allowed but not made compulsory.

1876    Before this time the ends were changed when a goal was scored. After this date, the teams only changed ends after half-time.

1880    One handed throw-ins.

1882    Throw-ins with both hands only.

Kinnaird played in nine Cup Finals. He was five times on the winning side, three times for the Wanderers, and twice for the Old Etonians. His mode of dress was well known: white flannel trousers and blue and white quartered cricket cap, and the appropriate shirt. He possessed a thick flowing beard of gingery red and was powerfully built.

Prior to 1872 he is believed to have picked both sides in the England/Scottish international matches. In the game played in February 1871 the England team mostly consisted of Wanderers players. The Scottish team comprised some interesting players including William Henry Gladstone MP, son of the Prime Minister (who like Kinnaird was a Liberal), Lord Kinnaird as expected and a certain Quintin Hogg. The game ended in a draw.

Kinnaird was always popular with the crowds, who once carried him to the players entrance. Always the extrovert, in 1882 he stood on his head after his team the Old Etonians had beaten Blackburn Rovers 1–0 in the final of the FA Cup at the Oval.

Like his family before him, Kinnaird continued their charitable ways. He was President of the YMCA and Lord High Commissioner to the Church of Scotland, and involved with numerous charities. Sadly he outlived five of his seven children and died two weeks after the death of his wife in 1923.

Cup Final attendance gradually increased. In 1878 it was 5,000; 1883, 8,000; 1889, 22,000; 1893, 45,000; and 1901, 110,000.

In 1873 the Royal Engineers made the first recorded football tour when they played friendly matches against Nottingham, Derby and Sheffield. A certain Sam Widdowson was to play for the Nottingham side, and was very impressed with the teamwork of the Engineers, so much so that he would later incorporate their style of play into his own side, Nottingham Forest.

Sam 'Weller' Widdowson (his father, Levi Widdowson, was a Dickens fan) was born in 1851 in Hucknall, Nottingham. He was involved in the lace trade, and in 1865 joined the firm of Messrs Jacoby. Initially his athletic career was based on running and hurdling, in which he excelled. He won approximately 300 trophies on the track. Sam was very keen on fitness, especially the use of weight training, which he used to build up his leg muscles. He was also to find this useful in football training. In 1869–70 he was to become involved (with his employer's family), in Nottingham Forest FC. Naturally his early pace was as useful in football as it was in running.

In 1873 he was made captain of the Nottingham Forest football team and remained so until he retired. One of the problems he was to encounter was the very rough play of some of the players. In 1874 he invented the shin guard, which was produced for him by F Boyington. The guard was worn outside the stocking.

He was also a fine cricketer, played for Nottinghamshire in 1878 and 1879, and was well known on local cricket grounds for many years playing for the Lace Manufacturers Eleven. In 1879 he was to marry Harriet Laslett, a tailor's daughter. Married life must have been good for Sam. In 1880 he was capped to play for England at soccer against Scotland together with his Forest colleague Edwin Luntley. The Forest team during that period included two other England internationals, Goodyear in 1879 and Sands in 1880. Tom Danks was to follow in 1885 (not to be confused with 'Dummy' Danks, Tom's deaf and dumb brother who also played for Forest).

Sam was always eager to improve his team's play and was the originator of the 2–3–5 formation. This in turn was copied by other leading clubs, and remained popular until the 1960s. Sam was a member of the FA Council from 1888–92.

In 1885 Forest reached the semi-final of the FA Cup for the third time. They played the Scottish Club Queens Park at Derby, the match being drawn 1–1; Tom Danks scored Forest's goal. Playing in goal that season for Forest was a player called Fred Beardsley. Fred was only 5 ft 7 in, but what he lacked in inches he made up for in agility and character. Had he been taller he would no doubt have been selected to play for England, and he was chosen to play in a representative match for Nottingham against London in 1884.

After the drawn semi-final match at Derby a replay was arranged in Scotland in the grounds of Merchiston Castle, Edinburgh. A large attendance was anticipated and a crowd of 14–15,000 duly arrived. Sadly for the Nottingham side it was not to be their day, as the Scots won the match by 3–0. Queens Park was at that time the best team in Scotland, and nearly all their team were Scottish internationals. In the match report, Beardsley was praised for his performance.

His employers, who gave him the sack for taking unauthorized leave, did not appreciate his achievement. This was the beginning of his wife Nellie's hate of football. That year they had an extra mouth to feed as son Fred junior was born. The family decided to move to Woolwich where Fred was to obtain work in the Dial Square factory in the Arsenal as a turner. His subsequent story is told in the remainder of this book.

# Chapter 1

David Danskin was born in 1863 in Burntisland, near Kirkcaldy ('lang toun', so called by the locals because there was once only one long street). David Danskin was his father's name and his father's before him. It was believed his surname was derived from one of his ancestors, who originated from Gdansk in Poland.

His father was a waterman. They lived in a cottage that was adjacent to a loch. In the school holidays he assisted his father by rowing around the local loch, while his father took the water level readings.

When he left school he became an apprentice engine fitter at the Kirkcaldy works. They were producing machines for marine engines, boilers and sugar and rice mills for the East and West Indies.

One of his worst memories was hearing of the Tay Bridge disaster on 28 December 1879. People had been travelling by train to their relatives for Hogmanay, when during a violent storm the bridge collapsed, taking the engine and five passenger carriages with it. Approximately 80 folk lost their lives.

There was unrest in the Highlands as this was the time of the 'Crofters war'. The landowners were able to make more profit from large-scale sheep farming. They were forcibly evicting the crofters, who were in turn retaliating against the landowners. In 1886 the crofters finally gained security of tenure.

There were problems at home. David had four sisters and they needed his room. He and his father did not always see eye to eye, so he decided to share a room with his friend James Henderson who was also an apprentice at the works. James's mother was a widow and took in lodgers. Jamie and he shared an enthusiasm for football. They both played for their local team, and being a hefty fellow, David usually played in defence. In the early 1880s he joined Kirkcaldy Wanderers.

Kirkcaldy Wanderers (1880–1901) was the town's first senior club. Suitable land was in short supply. They originally played at Robbies Park and Starks Park. In 1885 Kirkcaldy Wanderers joined with Kirkcaldy Rugby Club to form Kirkcaldy FC. The teams played on alternate Saturdays at Newton Park. In the summertime Kirkcaldy Cricket Club used the ground.

David was appointed captain in 1883, and played either halfback or goalkeeper when the need arose. In the main they used a 2–2–6 formation. They played in a smart all-white kit with a narrow red stripe on the outside leg of the knickerbockers.

Football was a vastly different game in those days. The defence consisted of the goalkeeper, who wore the same shirt as the rest of the team, and two defenders. Most of the play was in the goal area, and as a result of this six forwards were used. The goalkeeper used to be knocked into the goal as often as the ball. A normal ploy was for one of the two halfbacks to kick the ball into the opposing goal area. Then at least two forwards (who were onside when the ball was last played) would rush towards the goalkeeper to impede him if possible. Meantime, a further forward would slip past the scrimmage and hopefully score a goal. Corners were also a dangerous time for the goalkeeper. In those days very little heading of the ball was used because the ball was very heavy, especially in wet weather. The throw-in was officially changed to a two-handed throw-in in 1882. With the one-handed throw-in an experienced player could place a ball more accurately than with a free kick. It was about this time that some clubs first introduced rigid cross-bars instead of tapes.

There was no penalty area until the penalty kick was introduced in 1891. The goalkeeper was allowed to touch or bounce the ball within his own half but he was not allowed to run with the ball. From 1912 the goalkeeper was restricted to only handling the ball inside the penalty area.

Control of the game depended on the availability of people able to assist. In some of the earlier games it was left to the captains to adjudicate. Mostly, both teams would appoint an umpire, and each one would officiate only in the opposition's part of the pitch. The umpires signalled offences by waving white flags or handkerchiefs. Whistles were not normally used. In an important match, a third man would be appointed to act as timekeeper, and if there was a dispute he could give a casting vote. He would operate off the field of play.

On some occasions there would be a disputed result and a few bloody noses. At one match played on Stacks Park, a semi-final of the Kirkcaldy Junior Cup, much fighting broke out between supporters. In order to clear the pitch, Councillor Robert Stack, rope maker and owner of the ground, released a nearby bull on to the pitch and that had the desired effect! In Scottish football, the term 'Junior' denotes status, as opposed to age as in English football.

A newspaper report in the *Fife Free Press* dated 8 September 1883 describes Kirkcaldy Wanderers v Norton Park:

*On Saturday last the Wanderers first eleven journeyed to Edinburgh to open the ground of Norton Park FC. On the teams facing each other the home team opened the proceedings by kicking off, and for the first 20 minutes pressed the Wanderers rather severely, but were unable to score owing to the sure kicking of the backs and half-backs of the Wanderers who were in splendid form. At last the home team were rewarded by a well-taken goal from the foot of Adams. This reverse seemed to rouse the Wanderers, and their forwards getting possession of the ball took it smartly up to their opponent's goal, where it was put through out of a scrimmage. The Wanderer's had the home team completely hemmed in and succeeded in obtaining another goal, which left them the winners of a very fast game by two goals to one. Both teams played well all round.*

On the team list David Danskin is shown as captain and one of the halfbacks.

In his final years in Scotland, David was to meet both Peter Connolly and Jack McBean. They were also to play for Wanderers' first team. Little did he know he was to meet them again in the future.

A person who was to greatly influence his football career was John Smith, later Dr John Smith. He was born in Mauchline, Ayrshire (the village of Robert Burns) in 1855. As a schoolboy he played rugby. He first played 'soccer' (a term derived from 'association') because of a mistake. His rugby team arrived at an opponent's ground, only to find that a soccer team had been requested. Smith played soccer for Mauchline FC. Whilst studying medicine at Edinburgh University, he founded the university football team, continued to play for Mauchline, and was selected to play for Scotland against Wales in March 1877. In April 1879 he was reselected to play against England at the Oval, where Scotland lost 4–5. Smith scored one of Scotland's goals. Edinburgh University records state:

*J S Smith, of Mauchline is a very reliable forward, with rare speed, and a good dodger, passing judiciously. We have every reason to thank Mr Smith for having intro-duced the Association game to Edinburgh University. (SFA 1878–9)*

Smith was now a regular player in the university team, and played a further three times for his country in 1880–1, the most notable game being against England at the Oval, where Scotland beat England 6–1, with Smith scoring a hat-trick. Queen's Park, noting his talent, invited him to join their club. They were Scottish Cup winners in 1881 and 1884 and FA Cup finalists in 1884. Smith played in each of these matches. While with Queen's Park he played in three international games and scored each time. In 1884–5 he stopped playing Scottish football. While living in London he turned out for the Swifts, and appeared against Blackburn Rovers in an English FA Cup semi-final. Smith made his last appearance in association football in 1885/86, but ten years later went to Australia as manager of the Shaw-Shrewsbury British rugby team. For some reason he had to take the field himself, and closed his brilliant career the way he started – on the rugby pitch.

Dr Smith was a medical practitioner in Kirkcaldy and the local soccer clubs benefited from his coaching. They were also fortunate that he occasionally played for them as a halfback under the pseudonym of Miller.

Dr Smith was 6 ft 3 in tall and weighed 15 stone, but with his skills he did not have to rely on his brawn. He was a versatile athlete and an outstanding player of rugby, bowls, curling and golf. He died in 1934.

> On 5 September 1885, in the first round of the Scottish Cup, Arbroath beat Bon Accord, 36–0, a record for any first class British game. Bon Accord played in their normal working clothes and boots with a substitute goalkeeper who had never played in the position before; their usual goalkeeper having been taken sick. The Arbroath goalkeeper never touched the ball. John Petry scored 13 goals; on the same day Dundee Harp beat Aberdeen Rovers 35–0.

As a senior apprentice David was earning ten shillings a week in Kirkcaldy, but his training was nearing completion, and the practice was that when apprentices finished their indentures they were not normally required, as the pay for a journeyman was in excess of one pound a week. The employers were mostly reluctant to pay a newly qualified man £1 plus a week when they could acquire a very experienced worker for the same money, so it was common practice for young men to leave on completion of their apprenticeships and seek work elsewhere. After much deliberation and consultation with family and friends David decided, like many of his predecessors, to go to London with a friend. With much hugging and tears, he bade farewell to his family and the Hendersons. His father shook his hand and slipped an envelope into his pocket, which he rightly guessed contained a small cash sum, which helped sustain him in his early days.

It was a bright morning in 1885 when he made his way to London by various means of transport. London was a bleak and far dirtier city than he had envisaged, but there was an exciting, vibrant, pulsating feeling about it. To him the people appeared to be scurrying to and fro at approximately twice the speed of the people in Kirkcaldy. Of course in those days there were no cars. The horse-drawn bus and the hansom cab were the order of the day. Gas lighting was in vogue.

There were a high number of immigrants in the East End of London, including Jews who had made a mass exodus from Poland. Many of these had gone to the East End and joined Irish emigrants who had arrived earlier in the mid-nineteenth century, following the potato famine in Ireland.

> *The Irish emigrated to Britain and the United States, and in that period the population of Ireland fell by approximately 25 per cent. According to the 1851 census, 110,000 Irish immigrants had made their homes in London.*

Times were hard and there was general unrest and dissatisfaction everywhere in the British Isles, especially in Ireland where the population wanted home rule. The Independent Labour Party was founded in 1893, but it was not until 1919 that the first female MP was elected. The old and infirm were sent to the workhouses. The sexes were divided. The inmates of the workhouses were not paid but were provided with food and clothing in return for work, which usually consisted of picking oakum, fibre obtained by picking rope to pieces. This product was then used to seal the seams of ships.

> *An interesting story published in the* Kentish Mercury *gives some idea of the period. Henry Hayward, a painter, was in the employ of an Arsenal contractor. He lived at 22 Godfrey Street, Woolwich and was summoned to show*

*cause why he should not contribute to the support of his two daughters, Julia (aged 12) in the Girls Home, Swansea, and Eliza (aged 14) in the Cold Ash Industrial School, Newbury. The defendant said that two ladies at Aldershot had reckoned that they could get the girls into a good school, and he had allowed them to go. That was in May 1884. In the following February he found Julia ill in a small room with open windows and no fire. She had lost three toes from frostbite. He also saw Eliza, whose toes were frost-bitten. They were in a starving condition and were treated like convicts. He got Eliza away, but he was apprehended at Havant and fined £20 for assisting his daughter to escape from an industrial school. On his stating how he had been deceived, the fine was not enforced. His children had committed no offence and he wanted them home. The magistrate said defendants should apply to the Home Secretary. Hayward said he had done so but the Home Secretary replied he could not interfere. The magistrate said he would make the order for the lowest possible sum, namely six pence a week.*

Before David left home he was told he could obtain work in the Woolwich Arsenal armaments factory, where his knowledge of engines should be beneficial to him, and that proved to be the case. The Woolwich Arsenal complex was a large area of approximately 80 acres. It was originally a Saxon burial ground. Henry VIII was the first person to use the site for munitions, and manufactured gunpowder. David's workmates were an odd assortment of metal workers and engineers from all over the country. He worked in the Dial Square gun-finishing workshop. The buildings were used for turning, washing, engraving and finishing. The men's initial isolation was their common bond; they needed each other's comradeship. Many of them later married local girls. Luckily in those days there tended to be more women than men. David's wages in 1886 were approximately 35 shillings per week.

### Department of Employment Wages of Trades 1889
*Fitters and turners 38 shillings, 54-hour week.*
*Bricklayers: 9d an hour, average week 52½ hours.*
*Building labourers: 6d an hour, average week 52½ hours.*
*Skilled furniture workers: 9d an hour, 52-hour week.*

*Agricultural labourers: 13 shillings and 4d a week, hours
dependent on the time of year.*
*12d = one shilling, 20 shillings = one pound.*
*The word 'pound' was derived from a pound in weight of
silver, which used to make 240 silver pennies. The 'd'
came from the Roman word 'denarius'.*

There was great interest that year in the workshops regarding the
news of the discovery of gold in Witwatersrand in the Transvaal. Few
could envisage the ultimate misery this would cause the local inhabi-
tants, the Boers (Dutch farmers) or that it would lead to one of the
most shameful wars.

Strangely enough the British were then more concerned about war
with France, which for many centuries had been our main enemy, and
to a lesser degree the Spanish. Later we were to think of the Germans
as the aggressors and the French as our allies.

David rented various rooms in the area over the coming weeks, but
they were not very successful. They were either too gloomy or too
small, or he didn't like the other occupants. Then a colleague
suggested a woman who he knew had a room in St Mary Street.

The woman, Mrs Harradon, who was in her fifties, told David she
and her family had moved from Devon in search of work. Everything
had been going well when suddenly her blacksmith husband died.
Luckily by then her children were all in employment. She told him her
eldest daughter Georgina was a dressmaker who worked from home.
Her youngest daughter Henrietta had previously worked as a drapery
assistant. She was very proud of the fact that Henrietta had made a
good marriage, and had been blessed with a small family. She also had
a young servant girl to assist her. Henrietta's husband was Jonathan
Fletcher, a small businessman in the bakery and confectionery trade.
Mrs Harradon's youngest son Nicholas was a dairyman, which was
very handy because sometimes he was able to obtain dairy produce at
a reduced price.

They agreed the rent and David moved in the next day. He was
later to meet Georgina, often known as Georgie, and was soon smit-
ten with her, although she was some years older than him. Georgina
confided in him that the death of one of her sisters had devastated her
family, especially her late father who had been severely depressed for
several months and unable to work.

One afternoon in January 1884, Georgina told David, her brother
Nicholas had left their father lying on the couch and gone on his milk

round at 2 pm. When he returned at about 5.30 pm his mother asked him if he had seen his father, and as he had not, they decided to search the house and yard. Mr Harradon was found in an eight feet deep water tank containing about four and a half feet of water. Nicholas sought assistance from the Metropolitan Fire Brigade based next door, and Mr Tufnell, one of the firemen, helped to remove the body from the tank. Dr Fuller was called and arrived soon afterwards, and pronounced Richard Harradon dead. The coroner's jury later returned a verdict of suicide while 'labouring under temporary insanity'. Naturally, this put a terrible strain on the family, especially Georgina's mother.

In January 1886 Nicholas Harradon married Jane Hallam, the daughter of William Hallam, a foreman tailor, at All Saints Church. Three months later, on 7 April 1886, David was to marry Georgina at Mile End Registry Office. He was then 23, and she was almost 32. To save their mutual embarrassment his age was declared on the marriage certificate as 29 and hers as 30. They spent the next day in Greenwich. They visited the many attractions including the Observatory, the museum housing the model of the Battle of Trafalgar and the Nelson relics. Georgina enjoyed feeding the deer in the park.

When David returned to work the following day, he was greeted with the 'ringing-in' ritual for newly wed engineers. Colleagues were warned when the man was on his way in, and everyone in the shop got together to hit the boilers and plates of iron with their hammers. This clanging was kept going for about five minutes.

David and Georgina moved into lodgings in Brewer Street (now Wellington Street), in Woolwich. Their first bairn was born on 28 November 1886. His name was David Harradon Danskin. This followed the Danskin family tradition of calling the first-born son David, and of course Georgina's maiden name was Harradon.

David and Georgie were contented in their newly married life. The only thing lacking was David's unfulfilled desire to play football. He approached his work colleagues with the suggestion of forming a works team. The feedback was mixed, but most of the Scots were keen. There had previously been a football team at the works, but unfortunately it had failed through lack of support. They believed that with the increased popularity of football, they would be successful this time. The people in the south of England were mainly different from the Scots, inasmuch as in the summer cricket was the popular game, and in the winter rugby was played. They were amateur sports. Soccer was often frowned upon because of the emergence in the north of professionalism. In the past Alexander Smith, a turner, known as Joseph, had tried unsuccessfully to form a local team.

After discussions with his colleagues and consultations with the existing Dial Square cricket team, it was agreed that David should start a subscription list for a football team. Their new club was to be known as Dial Square, the name of their factory. The dial related to the sundial in the apex of the archway that was the entrance to their workplace.

The club really advanced when the men from the Midlands arrived: Bill Parr, Fred Beardsley and Charlie Bates from Nottingham, and Bob Crighton, Scottish born, with a Wolverhampton childhood. He had played for Wolverhampton Wanderers, who at that time wore red and white striped shirts with black knickerbockers. Nottingham Forest wore all-red shirts with white knickerbockers. Bob's younger brother Jim was also later to join the team.

Georgie meanwhile was nursing David junior, who sadly was a weak, sickly child. Prior to the birth she had been able to continue her dressmaking from home, so their financial situation was more secure than most of his work mates. David paid the balance outstanding for the first football.

The first game was to be on the Isle of Dogs on 11 December 1886. When they saw the pitch, they believed they should have used Dial Square's original name of 'The Great Pile'. The team was disappointed that Fred Beardsley would not be available as he was playing in the FA Cup for Nottingham Forest, in front of a crowd of 4,000 at Bramall Lane, Sheffield. The Nottingham umpire that day was a certain Joseph "Morris" Bates.

The Isle of Dogs pitch – if you could call it that – was a piece of wasteland (probably scrap land in Glengall Road, now Tiler Road), and because it was some distance away, the Dial Square team had not been able to prepare it. Their opponents were a team called Eastern Wanderers. The equipment consisted mainly of ordinary boots, with the addition of two or three bars across the sole and one across the heel. David wore shin pads outside his stockings. Knickerbockers were mostly worn with the stockings overlapping. Their shirts were of many colours, which was not a great problem, because having the same shirt in that period was not always a priority. In an England v Scotland International played in the same year, James Forrest, a half-back (the first professional to play for England) was forced to wear a different shirt from the rest of his teammates. Goal posts with rigid bars had been introduced in 1883, but on the Isle of Dogs the players used tapes, as the goal posts were mobile.

By the time the game was completed the pitch was a total quagmire; the players were coated in mud. The result was believed to be 6–0 to Dial Square.

After this first game the team decided to hold a meeting in the Royal Oak public house later in December. To be a successful football team, they needed to be better prepared for future fixtures. Their initial committee had already been appointed, and the first secretary was a local man, called Elijah Watkins but known as George.

They needed to find a suitable name for the team, draw up a fixture list and find a more local playing area. (There was a fine of ten shillings plus two shillings costs for playing unauthorized football on the common.) A more standard playing kit was another problem.

Caps had long been awarded to players in a variety of sports by public schools and universities. They were also awarded in international matches or representative games. This arose from the fact that footballers had worn a cap as part of their dress during the early years of the game. The cap and stockings were the main way of distinguishing the two teams before sides began wearing coloured shirts. Spectators could identify individual players by their caps long before the introduction of numbered shirts. Some early printed match cards, forerunners of the now familiar football programme, detailed the team line-ups accompanied by the colour of the cap that each player would wear for the match. Nottingham Forest players wore red caps. Caps were abandoned as soon as heading became a regular feature of the game.

Everton, founded in 1878, had a novel way of overcoming the problem of many different coloured shirts. They dyed them all black. For many years their nickname was 'the Black Watch'.

# Chapter 2

At the meeting in December of the Dial Square team, various proposals were discussed. It was interesting to see the emergence of potential leaders at this type of function.

## Football pitch

It was decided that their first playing area was to be on Plumstead Common, where the appropriate permission had to be obtained. The first season's matches were played there. A year later they approached a local pig farmer called 'Piggy' Walton, as they wished to obtain a more permanent soccer pitch, and asked him if he would allow them to rent a field near the Sportsman's public house, which was behind the Royal Ordnance Factory, close to the marshes. The field was sited amongst pigsties. 'Piggy' agreed but insisted they did not leave the goalposts erected, so Fred Beardsley kept them in his back yard.

It was agreed that at least one of the committee should supervise the condition of the pitch. Later, with Mr Walton's agreement, they decided to put ash down prior to match days to reduce the muddy conditions caused by the water from the marshes. Sadly it did not reduce the smell!

## Playing kit

Many of their early players were associated with Nottingham Forest. It was agreed to request their assistance in finding kit.

## Team name

There were already numerous sports teams playing under the name 'Royal Arsenal', including a rowing club, several cricket clubs and a football team using the elongated name of 'Royal Arsenal Gymnasium FC'. It was agreed that Dial Square sounded more like the name of a road, and they needed to widen the selection of players to other workshops in the Arsenal. It was decided to call the team plain 'Royal Arsenal'.

## Fixtures

'George' Watkins reported he had already been in touch with other clubs and had received encouraging replies.

## Umpires

Several men agreed to assist, including Jack Humble and Bill Parr.

Jack Humble, whose full name was John Wilkinson Humble, was a blunt speaking Yorkshireman, with a good brain and a rough sense of humour. He had walked to Woolwich with his brother Arthur. When the team converted into a company, Jack, like Fred Beardsley, was to become a director. Bill Parr was later to become the first team manager.

## Training

The lads from Nottingham were very experienced in training, especially in the use of weights, which helped to build up the team's leg muscles. They were left to organize the training programme.

## Tactics

Tactics had changed since David's early days in Scotland. Then his team had used two halfbacks, but fashions change, and Arsenal played with three halfbacks. The original function of the fullbacks was to make big kicks up to the six forwards, but in the latter part of the 1880s more emphasis was placed on passing and playing the offside rule. At that time, to prevent offside there had to be three defenders between the goal line and the opposition players when the ball was played. The rule changed in 1925 when this was reduced to two defenders.

## Transport

It was agreed that the team and some of the committee could travel in a 'brake', an open horse-drawn wagon, with seats, which was a very common early form of travel for football supporters. In Scotland they formed 'Brake clubs'. Another advantage of the wagon was that it could be used as a makeshift changing room if required.

When the meeting ended there was a general stampede for the bar. Everybody was filled with anticipation for the future.

Fred Beardsley occasionally made trips to Nottingham at the weekend. One day he returned with a ball and some second-hand Forest shirts. Everyone at the club was overjoyed with the gifts, although at that time they did not anticipate that there would be a price to be paid: Nottingham Forest would be requesting their cooperation for

**Royal Arsenal Football Team**
**First Eleven, season 1889–90**

*Middle row, left to right:* D Howat, J M Bates, J W Julian
*Bottom row, left to right:* R T Horsington, H Barbour, H Offer
*Back row, left to right:* P Connolly, J W Meggs, F W Beardsley, J McBean,
H R Robertson

Fred to be made available for crucial matches. Prior to Fred, Sands, an England international, had been Forest's goalkeeper. Fred had maintained that high standard, and at that time Forest were unable to find another goalkeeper of that calibre. In fact it was such a problem that when Fred was not available, the then veteran all-rounder Sam Widdowson had to be recalled to the side.

In Arsenal's early games they were only a small works team, but Nottingham Forest in a local derby against Notts County could muster a crowd of 10,000. You might wonder how Fred managed to get time off to go to Nottingham. Working conditions were then much different from today, and workers were employed on a much more casual hire and fire basis. It was accepted even in the Arsenal that whole departments could be closed for several weeks without pay when work was slack. Luckily for Fred, Arsenal's local bosses (who were army men) were very sports minded. Colonel Maitland was then in charge of the Dial Square factory.

Taking into consideration that there were then horse-drawn buses on the streets, and that Fred had to risk being unemployed, there had to be a good incentive besides glory for Fred, who was an astute businessman, to travel to Nottingham Forest's crucial games. At that time there was a good rail service to the Midlands, which helped enormously.

One of his colleagues was later to say about Fred, 'He would have been bumped out of the ground had he not been as agile as a cat. Good old Fred, a sturdy little chap, used to pitch opposing forwards over his back. He took it all. Now, the keeper has only got to be touched, and the whistle goes for a foul.'

One unusual experience that involved Fred took place on 9 April 1887. Nottingham Forest were playing away to Glasgow Rangers at Cathkin Park with an audience of 4,000. With ten minutes to go Forest were trailing 1–0. Fred attempted to catch a high ball, but fell clumsily and sprained his ankle. Almost immediately McLeod, a Forest fullback, also sustained a serious leg injury. Neither accident was attributed to foul play. While Fred was lying injured the ball remained in play, and the Rangers scored a second goal. Both the Forest players were then carried off. Naturally the Glaswegians, being perfect gentlemen, did not appeal for the second goal to be allowed. The game ended early, the result being 1–0 to the Rangers.

Fortunately for the Ordnance workers, during Queen Victoria's reign there were many minor wars. Britain's opponents included Maoris, Afghans, Zulus, Dervishes and Boers. The British Army still persisted in fighting in squares, a tactic that was effective against primitive races but not successful against more civilized forces. The first khaki uniforms were 'whites' that the soldiers had dyed with coffee and curry.

All Arsenal's initial matches were friendlies, and in their early seasons they were mainly successful against local clubs that consisted of local military units, churches, pubs and the like. Early notable opponents were Millwall Rovers, founded 1885, who later became Millwall Athletic FC. Like Arsenal, they were a works team. Their players mainly consisted of employees of Morton's jam and marmalade factory, and because they were mostly Scots they wore the blue national shirt. They were a strong side and the result was always unpredictable; they were able to give Arsenal the competitive edge they required to improve, and the same could be said of Tottenham Hotspur, which had been founded 1882, with the original name Hotspur FC. Arsenal's first competitive game was not until 18 October 1887, when they entered in the London Cup.

In order to maintain the high standards of the guns that Dial Square produced, they were periodically tested at Dover and Shoeburyness. Naturally there was an air of anxiety at the factory until these tests were finalised.

An extract from the *Kentish Mercury*, November 1886:

> *Some very interesting experiments took place on Thursday week, with the 80 ton guns at the turret on the Admiralty Pier, Dover, before the following committee of officers from Woolwich: - Sir F. Abel, Chemist to the War Department; Colonel Maitland, Superintendent Royal Gun Factory; Colonel Barlow, Superintendent Royal Laboratory; Major Ormsby, Royal Carriage Department; and Major Austrather, Artillery Department; with Colonel Noble, of the Gunpowder Factory. The object of the experiments was to test the general efficiency of the arrangements, particularly as to the working of the machinery used for loading the guns and revolving the turret. Altogether ten rounds were fired, the most ever fired at Dover at one time. The weather was beautifully fine, although a slight haze in the channel rendered it dangerous to adopt very long ranges. Previous to the guns being fired, a red flag was hoisted near the turret as a warning to the inhabitants on the seafront to open their windows in case of damage resulting from the concussion. The full charge of gunpowder was used, weighing 480 pounds, the weight of the shot being about 17 cwt.*

Arsenal founded their football team in the 'Days of *Gog*'. *Gog* was a purpose-built barge assembled in 1886 with rail track in the hold, which enabled the heavier guns to be wheeled on or off it. The barge was built to be towed by a war department tug. The guns were then taken to the appropriate destination for trials. *Gog*'s sister ship *Magog* was built in 1900.

That year Blackburn Rovers were to win their third successive Cup Final, which equalled the Wanderers record of the 1870s. Rovers beat West Bromwich Albion 2–0, after a replay.

1887 was a bad year for Georgie and David, since sadly it was the year of the death of their first bairn David. The poor sickly child succumbed to the inevitable in August.

---

**Royal Arsenal v Grove House, 8 October 1887**

In October Arsenal were supposed to have played their first round match in the London Cup against Grove House. Unfortunately Grove House were not able to bring their strongest team and conceded the match, but they did bring a 'scratch' side to play a friendly instead, which was lucky for Arsenal, as a crowd of approximately 500 had turned up to see their first 'competitive' match. They won the friendly 3–0.

---

In the next round Arsenal played Barnes who were a well-established London side. They were original members of the FA. The first Hon. Secretary of the FA was Captain E C Morley of Barnes. In 1868 four Barnes players represented Surrey against Kinnaird's Kent side: the match ended goalless. The match was played with 12 players on each side, and lasted 75 minutes with extra time of 15 minutes.

---

**Royal Arsenal v Barnes, 29 October 1887**

Arsenal were beaten by a much superior team 4–0. Fred played well: without him, no doubt they would have lost 10–0. Fred was devastated and not used to having four goals put past him. David blamed himself: he was of course one of the fullbacks, and since his injury had lost some of his pace. He offered to step down in future matches, but his colleagues refused to accept his offer. In forthcoming fixtures it was mutually decided that he should play as a halfback. The other fullback that day was Arthur Brown, another Nottingham man, who in later years was to become assistant secretary.

*Teams:*

**Royal Arsenal:** F W Beardsley, goal; A Brown and D Danskin (captain); backs; R Price, B Banks and T Wells, halfbacks; S Ridgewell, A Morris, C Bates, R Crighton and T Bee, forwards.

**Barnes:** E Mason, goal; L Morice (captain) and W E Muspratt, backs; A H Joyce, G E South and W E Timmis, halfbacks; A N Other, B Wilkinson, A Bathurst, E A Watson and A E Crews, forwards.

Umpires: W Parr (Royal Arsenal), H Bishop (Barnes). Referee: T Hudart (Erith).

---

For some time the Scottish FA had been annoyed that leading Scottish clubs were playing in the English FA Cup. By 1887 no less than seven Scottish teams had entered: Queens Park, Third Lanark, Heart of Midlothian, Renton, Rangers, Cowlairs and Partick Thistle, plus one from Ireland, Cliftonville of Belfast. That year the Scottish FA found the opportunity to object when Queens Park was drawn against Partick Thistle: an English cup tie being played by two Scottish sides in Scotland!

One memorable thing about the winter of 1887 was that it was intensely cold, and on the Prince of Wales pond in Blackheath, there was ice-skating. It was a bad year for the Ordnance factory as it had two fatalities. The first came from an explosion in the Royal Laboratory Department. Edward Prior of Turner Road, Lee, was using a mallet (which was the normal practice) in driving composition into tubes. He was producing rockets for the Royal Navy. A rocket exploded, one half hitting Prior, who died the next day.

The second death was at Dial Square where Henry Berry of Union Street, Woolwich, with another man, was moving a circular iron plate in the Turnery, when they lost their balance and it slipped to the floor. Berry had an iron plate weighing a ton fall upon him. They released him as quickly as possible and carried him to the Infirmary. His spine was broken in two places. At the inquest, it was said that three men normally carried out this work, but other witnesses said that on occasions two men were used. The Coroner heard that the deceased's wife had died five months earlier and he had left four orphaned children, the eldest of whom was 11.

1888 was an eventful year. Royal Arsenal FC moved grounds, the Jack the Ripper murders commenced and the match girls went on strike. Most importantly to the footballing public, the Football League was inaugurated. It was the brainchild of William McGregor, a Scot who was a committee member at Aston Villa. He initially wrote to five leading clubs proposing to form a league. This led to an exploratory meeting at Anderson's Hotel, Fleet Street in March 1888. The first teams consisted of:

*Accrington, founded 1878, holders of the Lancashire Cup.*

*Aston Villa, founded 1874, formerly a chapel team called Villa Cross (FA Cup holders 1887).*

*Blackburn Rovers, founded 1875, three times winners of the FA Cup, 1884/85/86.*

*Bolton Wanderers, founded 1874, formerly a Sunday school team called Christ Church Bolton.*

*Burnley, founded 1882, formerly Burnley YMCA.*

*Derby County, founded 1884, home of the Shrove Tuesday games 500 plus per side 'Derby Match'.*

*Everton, founded 1878, formerly St Domingo's Church Sunday School.*

*Notts County, founded 1862, the oldest league side. Elected to the annoyance of Nottingham Forest.*

*Preston North End, founded 1881. First League champions, 'The Invincibles'.*

*Stoke, founded 1863, later Stoke City FC.*

*West Bromwich Albion, founded 1879, formerly West Bromwich Strollers. FA Cup runners-up 1887, winners 1888.*

*Wolverhampton Wanderers, founded 1877, formerly Boys at St Luke's Church Blakenhall (who later merged with Wanderers FC 1880).*

The first League champions were Preston North End, 'the Invincibles'. They won the championship without losing a match. Their league record was played 22, won 18, drawn 4, goals for 74, goals against 15, points 40. They were also successful in the 1888–9 FA Cup. They won their fifth round tie against Aston Villa 3–1 in front of a record crowd of 27,000. In the final they beat Wolverhampton Wanderers 3–0. The referee was Major Marindin. They were the first team to achieve the League and FA Cup double. Their win in the first round of the FA Cup against Hyde in 1887–8 by 26–0 is still a record. E C Bambridge, the England international who had played against the 'Invincibles' on various occasions, was to comment that 'Preston's strength lay in the fact that they dovetailed together.'

Preston were way ahead of their time in making the game more professional. They attracted quality players by offering them good jobs, and introduced a rigorous training programme. Their Chairman and Manager was Major William Sudell, and he was responsible for enticing many good players to Preston, including their star centre forward Johnny Goodall (known as Johnny Allgood) and Nick Ross.

**Royal Arsenal v Clapton, 19 January 1889**

This semi-final tie in the London Association Senior Challenge Cup took place at Leyton. It was a stubbornly contested game throughout, with Clapton generally having the best of it. Cowan and Connell scored, and together with Casselton, Clark and Prior were the dominant players in the Clapton side. For the Arsenal, Beardsley and the backs played well, and Scott and Morris were noticeable among the forwards. The final score was Clapton 2, Arsenal 0.

**Royal Arsenal** team: F W Beardsley, goal; J B Crighton and J McBean, backs; A Brown, J M Bates and D Danskin, halfbacks; A J Morris, and R Crighton, right wing; P. Connolly, centre; J M Charteris and W Scott, left wing.

David finished this game with a slight limp and decided that from now on, he would be prepared for others to take his place. He continued to play on rare occasions. The two Crighton brothers made the same decision.

# Chapter 3

1889 was an important year for the Woolwich club, as it was their first year in the FA Cup. Locally there was more worker rebellion. David's sister Magdalene married James Berry, a shepherd. He had thought she would remain a spinster, but she surprised everyone. She was 27, her groom 29. David's father was promoted to manager of the local water works.

On 2 February 1889, Fred Beardsley played for Forest against Linfield Athletic of Ireland, at home in the first round proper of the FA Cup. Nick Ross of the Preston Invincibles had coached Linfield in the summer. The game finished disastrously, 2–2 after extra time, and that meant Forest had to travel to Ireland for the replay. On arrival in Belfast they were informed that the Irish team had scratched because they had fielded an ineligible player in the first game. It was therefore decided to play a friendly, which Forest lost 3–1 in front of a crowd of 6,500.

The Irish press saw the match in a different light. Extracts from the *Ulster Cyclist and Football News*, Friday 15 February 1889:

> *The game was watched with great interest and when at call of time Linfield were the conquerors by 3–1, the excitement of the spectators knew no bounds. The Sprinters were cheered and chaired over the ground, but the spectators, to put it figuratively, 'hallowed before they were out of the woo,' for scarcely was the whistle blown ere a rumour was flying round the field like wildfire that Linfield had scratched to Forest, and that the so called tie was merely a friendly match. When the rumour received confirmation footballers were highly incensed at being tricked into witnessing a sham cup tie, and wasting their enthusiasm on the desert air, and rightly so, as no one cares to be taken in, which the spectators undoubtedly were at Ballynafeigh, and it would have been much better for all parties concerned had the fact been announced before the game commenced. Had this been done the spectators would not have had to leave the ground with the idea hammered into them that they were deluded.*
>
> *The reason given why the Linfield secretary did not inform the football public of the team having scratched to*

*Forest, was in deference to the wishes of Mr Widdowson, the vice-president of the Nottingham club, who requested that the matter be kept from both teams, and let them play a cup tie game.*

*Mr Gordon, the Linfield secretary, informed us that not a single member of the Linfield team was aware that the game was not a cup tie, and anyone who saw the 'Sprinters' play can well believe it, but not so the Forest. Every man of the eleven must have known of the arrangement, as the play at goal was lackadaisical in the extreme, and anyone watching them coming up the steps of the pavilion after the match would have guessed from the expression of their countenance that their defeat was not troubling them to any great degree.*

Compensation for Linfield was that they were to win the Irish Cup three times, in 1890–1, 1891–2 and 1892–3.

In the next round Forest were drawn against Chatham, and after two replays were beaten 3–2 at the Kennington Oval (a neutral ground). This was the last occasion that Fred would play for the Nottingham side, much to the relief of his long-suffering wife Nellie. Chatham was hammered in the next round 10–1 by the powerful professional league side West Bromwich Albion.

Fred had the taste for high-class football and urged the committee to enter the Arsenal team for the FA Cup, which they duly did.

The heaviest defeat Arsenal suffered during the 1888–9 season was at the hands of Boston Town in an Easter friendly match. Interestingly, the pre-match report in the edition of the *Boston Guardian* dated 18 April 1889 lists the Woolwich Arsenal team as 'a very strong eleven' comprising Beardsley (Nottingham Forest), goal; McBean (Kirkcaldy Wanderers), Wilson (Huddersfield), backs; Howat (Preston), Bates (Nottingham Forest) and Brown (Notts Rangers), halfbacks; Horsington (Swindon Town) and Connolly (Kirkcaldy Wanderers) right wing; Barbour (Third Lanark and Lincoln City), Charteris (Everton) and Scott (Notts Rangers), left wing. Boston Town, known as the 'Black and Tans', played in their normal black and amber narrow striped shirts.

**Boston v Royal Arsenal, 19 April 1889**
This match was the first of three specially arranged for the Easter holidays, and was played on the Lord Nelson ground on Good Friday.

The weather was perfect. No fewer than 1,200 spectators gathered round the ropes, the grandstand being filled to its full capacity. The captain of the home team won the toss and elected to kick into the High Street goal with the wind and sun in the rear. The game started fast, both goals being under siege. Horsington and Connolly attacked briskly on the right wing. Connolly dribbled past Jeffrey and sent in a stunning shot that Gresham cleared in brilliant style, fisting it over the cross-bar but giving away a fruitless corner, Boston then contested well and Julian moved into the goal area. He then passed to Stubbins who missed the opportunity to score.

The home men continued to press, and obtained a corner, which was cleared, but Geeson collected a loose ball and passed to Smith whose shot struck the bar. The game continued at high speed, neither side gaining any advantage until Boston gained a free kick, from which they failed to score. After half an hour's play Milnes rescued Jeffrey who mishit his goal kick, and from a long ball to Price, the forwards obtained a corner off Wilson. This was well centred, Geeson, Smith and Curtis all shooting, but Beardsley saved well until 'Pickles' Smith evaded him by scoring with a ground shot in the corner. Boston continued to have the best of the play, and Beardsley, catching the ball from the toe of Curtis, was kicked in the stomach by Beales. The referee promptly gave a foul. The free kick relieved the pressure on the Arsenal goal, and half-time was then called, when the game stood at 1–0 to Boston.

After the usual interval the Woolwich men pressed and obtained a free kick from a foul by Julian. This was badly placed down the field and from it Stubbins broke away and shot, but the keeper saved. Agar, Smith and Geeson had repeated tries for a goal, but Beardsley cleared. Minutes later Beales obtained the ball from a centre by Smith after a throw-in, and scored. Arsenal pressed forward and after some resolute work in front of the home goal, which kept the goalkeeper and backs under pressure, Meggs scored for the Reds: Arsenal 1, Boston 2. Boston was granted a corner, and half an hour from the restarting, Agar touched the ball to Curtis and he crossed to the left from which Geeson scored 3–1. Ten minutes later Smith added another goal to the score, and thus the game ended, the home team winning 4–1.

*Teams:*

**Boston:** Gresham, goal, Milnes and Jeffrey, backs, Julian, Price and Argar, halfbacks, Stubbins and Beales, right wing, Smith and Geeson, left wing, and Curtis, centre.

The **Royal Arsenal** team was as shown in the pre-match report above, except that Meggs played instead of Scott.

Julian, having been approached by Arsenal, left Boston to join his new team almost immediately after the match on Good Friday. The *Boston Guardian*, in its Football Notes on Saturday 4 May 1889, stated 'at the end of the season a heavy affliction has fallen on Boston Football. Julian the Captain, the best fellow and the best player in the team, has left us to go to Woolwich Arsenal. The Secretary of the Arsenal FC spotted him on the now fatal Good Friday. Work at 50 shillings a week was obtained for him in the Arsenal and Julian left us on Saturday night. I do not blame him for going, but his loss is a heavy and sore one.'

Bill Julian as a teenager

This report conflicts with another printed in the *Boston Guardian* on 18 April 1889, where it was rumoured that Julian might retire from the game at the end of the season. It was hinted that this decision was due to Julian being henpecked. This was later strongly denied by his family.

Julian arrived in Plumstead with an army of relatives. On the first floor of number 195 Plumstead High Street lived Bill Julian with his wife Edith, sister Alice and baby son Joseph. On the ground floor lived his sister Mary with her husband Josiah Wallis, an engine fitter, and their four children. Bill Julian was popular with both the committee and players. He was later appointed team captain. His best position was centreback. Like Morris Bates he was proficient at heading the ball.

He was to tell of some interesting incidents that he had witnessed at football matches. In 1887 during a Lincoln City v Gainsboro match, a spectator was smoking a wooden pipe. He was struck in the face by the ball and the stem of the pipe went through his cheek. In an FA Cup-tie played at Trent Bridge between Notts County and Queens Park, a spectator trying to get a good view fell from a tree and broke his ribs.

New players of quality in the Arsenal team included:

**James William Meggs** (forward), a local born in Lewisham. He came from a footballing family, his brother George also being a useful inside forward.

**Henry Thomas Offer** (fullback) was born in Devizes, a joiner by trade. His daughter Ethel was later to marry a professional footballer.

**Richard Thomas Horsington** (forward), an engine fitter by trade, joined with Offer from Swindon.

**Humphrey Barbour** (forward) was born in Glasgow, the son of a policeman, and a turner by trade.

**David Howat** (right half), born in Preston of Scottish parents. He became a fitter in Dial Square. His mother's family were drapers in Preston.

**Hope Robertson** (inside forward), born in Whiteinch, Lanark, was originally a rivet heater employed in the shipbuilding industry. His previous club was Partick Thistle.

Other matters of interest that year were the strike by artillery drivers at the Woolwich garrison, the dock strike, and unrest and dissatisfaction at the Southwark and Deptford Tramways Company. Naturally, none of the locals expected the military to take action. All this insurrection was probably due to the success of the match girls' strike the previous year.

Report by the *Kentish Mercury*, 13 September 1889:

> ### Insubordination of Troops at Woolwich. Artillery Drivers on Strike
>
> *Some excitement has been caused in the garrison at Wool-wich by the insubordination of all the drivers of the 6th Field Battery Royal Artillery (late 8 Battery, 2nd Brigade), quar-tered at the Grand Depot Barracks. It appears that some dissatisfaction has existed amongst the drivers, who allege that they are unnecessarily harassed and overworked, it being, they say, the general rule for the drivers of the 6th Battery to be in the stables after the men of other batteries have left. On Saturday the battery, which is a smart one, was present at the inspection of troops by the Duke of Cambridge on Woolwich Common, and the drivers were at work in the stables till about four o'clock. Subsequently, the commanding officer of the battery ordered an inspection of harness for Sunday, and there was also an order for a marching order parade on Monday. The men say that the inspection of harness was unnecessary, and resolved to strike. On Monday, when they should have got ready for the marching order parade, the whole of the drivers, some 88 in number, marched direct, without any orders, to the guard room, where they were placed under arrest. Subse-quently the majority of them were released, about a dozen of the ringleaders, and those who remained obdurate, being detained for trial by court-martial, the evidence for which is now being prepared. On Tuesday an inquiry took place before officers of the regiment, and other investigations were being made on Wednesday when there were nearly 20 men under arrest. The number was increased by similar insubordination on the part of individual men who, being requested to do work which they did not like, would march to the guardroom. On account of the drivers refusing to work the gunners of the battery are, of course, disabled from doing any work with the guns.*

In September Arsenal played Tottenham Hotspur in a friendly; the previous games had been close but on current form they thought they

shot at goal, which Lemarchand, who was waiting just in front of the goal, headed in. An appeal was made for offside but the goal was allowed. With only 12 minutes to play, and two goals down, matters looked none too bright for the Reds, and the spectators seemed to give up hope. This was not so however with the players, who pressed forward. After some good passing, Robertson scored for the home team amidst tremendous cheering. Connolly, who had just changed places with Barbour, led his men on at great speed, and the game became very exciting, the Reds doing most of the attacking. Scott scored a second goal five minutes before time amidst great enthusiasm. A corner was awarded to the Arsenal but produced no goal. The game ended in a 2–2 draw.

By the rules of the Football Association, it was compulsory to play an extra half-hour. The referee recommended that both captains protest on account of the bad light, but both sides were anxious to have the game settled, so it was decided to play on. When the game resumed, the Reds went off at great speed and it could be seen that they were in better condition than the Crusaders, who began to tire. From a clearance by Coulby, Connolly dashed up and scored, and keeping up the pressure, Meggs added another goal.

The Crusaders returned the attack on the home goal, which Foster kept intact, but two minutes before time, the Reds' forwards, broke away and Robertson scored the third goal. When the whistle blew, the undefeated Arsenal retired victors 5–2. For the Arsenal, all the halfbacks played a fine game. Connolly, Scott and Robertson were also prominent. Amongst the visitors the brothers Lawrence at back played well, and Pike was the best of the forwards.

*Teams:*

**Royal Arsenal:** R Foster, goal; P Connolly and J McBean, backs; D Howat, J M Bates and J W Julian, halfbacks; J W Meggs, J M Charteris, H Barbour, H R Robertson and W Scott, forwards.

**Crusaders:** G A Coulby, goal; H C Lawrence and G H Lawrence, backs; T W Gallibrand, B Blount and A M Daniel, halfbacks; W G Connell, A W Lemarchand, E C Evelyn (captain), T M Pike and F H Stevens, forwards.

Umpires: Comerford and Jackson. Referee: T Gunning, Hon Sec London Football Association.

The Corinthians football team was founded in 1882 at the suggestion of N L Jackson who wished to give England players the experience of playing together, following repeated defeats by Scotland. The team occasionally included non-English players. Evelyn was a Welsh international. A M Daniel later became a director of the National Gallery. He was rewarded with a knighthood.

Arsenal's next FA Cup fixture was against the Swifts. The Swifts were an established celebrity eleven comprising football internationals and players of the highest quality. Past players included Dr John Smith, the Scottish international, and the three Bambridge brothers who had all played for England: Arthur, Ernest, a member of the Stock Exchange, and Edward Charles, a member of Lloyd's. Edward, known as 'Charlie Bam', commenced his international career as a teenager and played 18 times for England. He was a small man and weighed only 8 st 5 lb the first time he played for England. He was always cheerful and an outstanding outside left. In one international he scored a hat-trick.

**Corinthians, 1887**
*Top row (left to right):* A Walters, Cobbold, Amos, N Jackson, Saunders, Brann, Mills-Roberts
*Bottom row (left to right):* Challen, P Walters, Bayley, Tinsley, Lindley, E C Brambridge

Charlie Bam was due to play in a County Cup final but had unfortunately broken a leg some weeks before, and it was assumed by the rival team that he would not attend. To their utter dismay, he turned up at the last minute, changed and ready to play, wearing a white shin guard on one leg, which was soon covered in marks. Despite this rough treatment, Bambridge managed to score the winning goal, and it was later discovered that the shin guard had been placed on his good leg as bait. Using this tactic his weakened leg was unharmed.

In this particular fixture the Swifts were to field four internationals, Saunders, Brann and Swepstone for England and Lambie for Queens Park and Scotland, and maybe one more, as a spectator believed he had overheard one of the Swifts address E C 'Lloyd' as Charlie. Of course Bambridge worked for Lloyd's. Swifts' all-white kit contrasted well with Arsenal's bright red shirts. There was a snowstorm beforehand, but the committee of the Royal Arsenal FC had the snow cleared from the field of play, and although the ground was heavy the 6,000 spectators who lined the ropes witnessed a good game.

**Royal Arsenal v Swifts, 7 December 1889**

The Swifts played resolutely from the kick-off, and before three minutes had elapsed, Lambie had scored; the goal however was doubtful, but was allowed. Connolly and Julian with Robertson and Barbour pressed Swepstone, and two shots from Barbour resulted in a corner. Brann and Lloyd broke away and 'hands' was given in front of the Arsenal goal. Connolly removed the danger. A few minutes later, Brann struck a good goal for the visitors. The Arsenal then pressed forward but had hard luck in having the ball just miss the goal, Swepstone on another occasion kicking away when scoring seemed a certainty. However, just before half-time, Meggs from a pass by Barbour scored Arsenal's first goal.

In the second half the Swifts started brightly, but the Reds seemed to tire. Offer had his knee out, and Howat's ankle gave way, while Meggs had a sprained leg, so matters were not of the brightest for the locals. Hogarth and Lambie kept pressing, but Foster played a great game in goal, warding off the powerful forwards with determined skill. However 'Lloyd', Hogarth and Brann found opportunities to score, Brann's goal, though doubtful, being allowed. This was strongly disputed by the Arsenal supporters behind the goal. The last quarter of an hour found the Reds once more attacking, but Wells and Haldane-Stewart were equal to the occasion, and time was called with the score standing at Swifts 5, Arsenal 1. Lambie, Brann, Saunders and Hogarth were the best of the Swifts; Foster, Barbour, Julian, and Connolly being the pick of the locals.

*Teams:*

**Royal Arsenal:** R Foster, goal; P Connolly, and J McBean backs; H Offer, D Howat and J Julian, halfbacks: J W Meggs, W Stewart, H Barbour, H Robertson and E Williams, forwards.

**Swifts:** H A Swepstone, goal; W C Wells and R Haldane-Stewart, backs; F E Fernie, F E Saunders and C Sanderson, halfbacks; E C 'Lloyd', G Brann, J W Summerhayes, J A Lambie and R G Hogarth, forwards.

As previously mentioned, occasionally workers in various sections of Woolwich Arsenal were laid off. When this happened money was in short supply. To help out the first port of call would be the pawnbroker, where people could pawn items of clothing, bedding, and tools and so on for a few shillings to tide them over. Where there was a prolonged shut down, and there was no money to pay the rent, it was common practice to do a 'moonlight flit': remaining possessions were put into a handcart and removed to new lodgings. In David's case, Georgie would go round to her brother-in-law Jonathan the baker and scrounge any leftover bread. She was always fond of saying how fortunate they were to be able to rely on Jonathan. Although David was grateful for her family's assistance, he also found it embarrassing that he could not always make ends meet. Imagine his surprise when in December, Jonathan was convicted in the Woolwich police courts for driving a cart which did not display his name and address. For this offence he was fined two shillings plus two shillings costs. Georgie was horrified, but David was ashamed to feel a little bit of smug satisfaction at the outcome.

In 1890 the Irish and Scottish Leagues were formed, and in the FA Cup Final Blackburn Rovers beat Sheffield Wednesday, with Blackburn's Townley scoring the first hat-trick in an FA Cup final. Goal nets were invented. Several new faces appeared at Arsenal: William Campbell, William George, David Gloak, Thomas Pell and John Sheppard.

The Woolwich free ferry caught fire and there was more industrial unrest. Shop workers were allowed to close early on Wednesday at 5 pm instead of working the normal 8 am to 10 pm shift.

In March 1890 Arsenal reached the Final of the London Association Cup, following wins over Marlow (4–1) and the Second Battery of the Scots Guards (3–0). In the final they were to meet Old Westminsters.

Old Westminsters' star players were their England internationals, Ralph Squire, equally good at fullback or halfback, and 'Billie Moon', their goalkeeper. Ralph had originally played for Cambridge; he was appointed their captain in 1886. They were both members of the Corinthians. G O Smith, the England international and friend of Billy Moon, was later to say that he was a sturdy goalkeeper, who gave as good as he got in the matter of charging, and was also very quick at foreseeing where a shot would come from. Smith and Moon played together and against each other on countless occasions, and in a match between Old Carthusians and Old Westminsters they collided head to head. Smith was knocked unconscious but his head broke Moon's cheekbone and smashed the retina of his eye. Fortunately the eye damage healed. Moon occasionally kept wicket for Middlesex but played cricket mostly for the Hampstead Club. He was a solicitor by profession and belonged to the same London club as Smith.

Billy Moon

Up to within a few days of the match, the Arsenal supporters were confident that their team would complete the season's triumph by landing the championship of the London District. The record of the Arsenal since October had been one of consistent success, and generally it had been looked upon as the coming club. On the night before the match, everything pointed to a fast game, the Oval ground being in excellent condition. Steady rainfall early on Saturday morning dispelled any hopes of playing on a fast ground. As early as 1 pm, enthusiastic Arsenal supporters started to gather around the ropes, and by 3 pm all the best positions outside the barriers as well as the banks had been occupied. There must have been well over 6,000 spectators. Old Westminsters wore their usual red and white halved shirts.

### Royal Arsenal v Old Westminsters, The London Association Cup, 8 March 1890

Just before 3.30 pm, the two teams entered the field. A strong breeze was blowing directly down the ground to the gas works, making the choice of ends vital. Old Westminsters lost the toss and Squire, their captain, marshalled his men in the eastern half with the wind blowing in their faces. They kicked off spot on 3.30 pm. There was a hearty cheer from their supporters following Veitch, Probyn and Street's quick neat passing till they reached the Arsenal goal area. The frequent gusts added considerably to the difficulties of the Westminsters' backs, and the strength of Fox and Squire was more than neutralized by the wind, which constantly carried the ball over their heads. Meggs and Horsington were combining well on Arsenal's right wing until Horsington sustained an injury, which reduced his pace.

Each time Bain received the ball, there was a thrill of expectancy from the old boys' fans. They were not disappointed. His brilliant dribbles on the left kept the Reds occupied. Julian, Howat and McBean showed good defence for the Arsenal, but the superior weight and pace of the Westminsters gave them the edge. Bain put in a hot shot that sent the ball whizzing outside the right post of the Arsenal goal. With the help of the wind, the Woolwich forwards had several times been close to scoring, although in each case their efforts were frustrated by Moon, whose defence was brilliant throughout. Offer very nearly headed the ball between the Westminsters' posts and soon after, Moon was just in time to prevent Robertson scoring from a very good shot. The Westminsters' forwards were never idle, with Bain, Veitch and Street leading the attack. Bain's ball control was excellent and at last his efforts were successful. Street, to whom the ball had been passed, sent

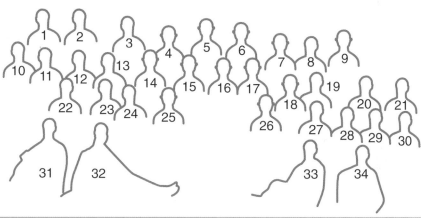

**Royal Arsenal, 1890**

Key:

| | | | |
|---|---|---|---|
| 1 Singleton | 10 Connolly | 19 Danskin | 28 Walton |
| 2 Campbell | 11 Horsington | 20 George | 29 Gardener |
| 3 Christmas | 12 Howat | 21 Fry? | 30 Morgan |
| 4 not known | 13 McBean | 22 Beardsley | 31 Barbour |
| 5 not known | 14 Parr | 23 Julian | 32 Scott |
| 6 Reed | 15 not known | 24 Bates | 33 Stewart |
| 7 Jackson | 16 Stewart | 25 Davis | 34 Grandison |
| 8 Wilson | 17 Humble | 26 not known | |
| 9 Gloak | 18 Ogleby | 27 Brown | |

it between the Arsenal posts just out of Beardsley's reach. This goal was scored only 20 minutes from the kick-off, and a few minutes later Horsington was injured for the second time and took no further part in the match. He was sorely missed.

In spite of the good defence of Julian, Connolly and McBean, the Westminsters kept up a vigorous attack, and twice Street was dangerously close to scoring another goal. At last the Arsenal rallied and became the attackers, and Barbour, Offer and Meggs were untiring in their attempts to break through the defence of Fox and Squire. A fine centre by Meggs into the mouth of the Westminsters' goal was allowed to escape, and just before half-time, Moon saved his side in most brilliant style by stopping what appeared to be an almost certain goal from a free kick for 'hands'.

The change of ends in the second half did not prove so beneficial to the Westminsters because the sun came out and the wind had dropped, and consequently the Arsenal were not faced by the same difficulties encountered by the Westminsters. During the early part of this half, Barbour and Meggs were most prominent for the Arsenal team, and Moon twice had some trouble in protecting his goal. Then for a period Old Westminsters kept the ball mostly in the opposite half. A fast run by Veitch ended with an excellent shot that Beardsley smartly stopped. Just after this Moon too was pressed, but he was never in difficulty and he generally cleared the ball before there was any real danger. Towards the end of the game, there was roughness among some of the players on both sides. The last 15 minutes of the game was occasionally exciting, but the Old Westminsters' defence was equal to the Arsenal attack, and at the end of the game, the score was 1–0 to Old Westminsters.

*Teams:*

**Old Westminsters:** W R Moon, goal; C J Fox and R T Squire, backs; H Wetton, W N Winckworth and H Harrison, halfbacks; P C Probyn and H O Peck, right; J G Veitch, F W Bain and F Street, forwards. F Street was sadly killed in the First World War.

**Royal Arsenal:** F W Beardsley, goal; P Connolly and J McBean, backs; D Howat, J M Bates and J W Julian, halfbacks; R T Horsington and J W Meggs, right; H Barbour, centre; H R Robertson and H Offer, left, forwards.

Umpires: F Barnett (Vice-President, London Football Association) and F J Wall (Rangers). T Gunning (Hon Sec London Football Association) was referee.

The locals felt that the Old Westminsters were fortunate to have the services of William Moon who was the current England goalkeeper. The previous year both Scotland and Wales had had much difficulty in scoring against him, losing 5–0 and 5–1. With Arsenal losing a forward for most of the game it was not surprising that they failed to score. Many thought that with a full squad, Arsenal would have the beating of the Old Westminsters, and there was an air of expectancy for the rematch in the London Charity Cup in April.

# Chapter 4

Jimmy Hill, a veteran of the early Arsenal team, was to recommend Albert Christmas, a promising right winger. Albert was born in Villiers Street, Blakenhall in 1868. Like Jimmy a tin worker by trade, he attended St Lukes School (forerunner of Wolverhampton Wanderers FC). At the age of 15 he was spotted by Fergus Hill, a Wolves official, father of Jimmy, and was given a trial in the third team. The next week he was promoted to the second team, joining his older brother Harry. In 1886 Albert was selected to play for the first team. Although he was obviously highly skilled, there were members of the committee who felt he was a bit fragile, being 6 feet tall but weighing only 10 stone (the average player was approximately 2 stone heavier). Albert was so fast that defenders had difficulty in putting in a hard tackle. He also had the habit of kicking the ball through his opponent's legs, and much to the amusement of the crowd, then did the splits. This did not endear him to his opponents.

Wolves became so concerned regarding his safety that they employed a local ex-boxer, Len Evans, who used to mingle with the crowd, and then run on the pitch at the first sign of any possible violence to him.

Albert played for Wolves in an exhibition match against Kidderminster. After he had scored three goals, the Wolves secretary reminded him that this game was only an exhibition match and that they did not wish to offend Kidderminster. A few months later Kidderminster Olympic requested that Wolves lend them a few players, including Albert. Wolves obliged, and Albert and a back called Oldershaw were sent to Olympic. Sadly Oldershaw was to drop dead during the match.

In early 1890 Albert became unemployed and was offered work at the Royal Arsenal provided he played for the team. When he arrived he was immediately installed in the first team.

That year Kidderminster Olympic wrote to Albert asking him if he would play for them in the Weavers Cup Final against Kidderminster Harriers. When he returned he found streamers and placards everywhere proclaiming 'Christmas is coming'. Olympic was to win the final 5–1. As usual Albert was amongst the scorers.

That year Albert was selected to play for the London FA v Sussex at Brighton.

While at Woolwich, Albert was often to be seen riding his penny-farthing bicycle. He was a cycling enthusiast, and when he was in the Midlands he had won two handicap races at the Lower Aston grounds.

In March Arsenal reached the final of the Kent County Senior Cup, in which they were to play Thanet Wanderers at Chatham. David Danskin felt this competition was a pointless exercise. In the earlier rounds the club had won its fixtures by 6–1, 10–1, 7–2 and 5–0.

> **Royal Arsenal v Thanet Wanderers, 22 March 1890**
> With the wind behind them during the first half, many expected the Royals to build up a big lead, but in fact by half-time they were leading by only one goal to nil, scored by Barbour. In the second half the Wanderers attacked strongly, but thanks to the good defence of Connolly and McBean they failed to score. At the other end, Offer's shot hit the post, and again the Royals broke away, with Offer scoring a second goal from a clever pass by Robertson. A few minutes later Barbour was to score a third. The final result was 3–0 to Arsenal.
> Team:
> **Royal Arsenal:** F W Beardsley, goal; P Connolly and J McBean, backs; D Howat, J M Bates and J W Julian, halfbacks; H Offer and H R Robertson, left wing, H Barbour, centre, J W Meggs and A Christmas, right wing forwards.

Bill Julian's union card

Because of the heavy fixture list Danskin was asked to keep goal against Clapton in a friendly game. This game reunited the old Kirkcaldy Wanderers defence of McBean, Connolly and Danskin. The former England goalkeeper and ex-Pilgrims player Harry Swepstone played in goal for Clapton.

**Clapton v Royal Arsenal, 28 March 1890**
A crowd of about 2,000 assembled on this Saturday at the Spotted Dog Ground at Upton to see the game between the strong southern teams. The Royal Arsenal was without Julian, Bates, Meggs and Beardsley, and Clapton was without Casselton. The game was well contested throughout; play was fast and fairly even, and Clapton added another to their list of victories winning 2–0. It must be said that the Arsenal were unfortunate in failing to score, and they were disadvantaged in losing the services of Offer at the interval, this player having to leave through a leg injury. Shortly before the interval a well-judged shot by Smith gave Clapton their first goal. Danskin should have fisted away, but he failed to fully grasp the ball, and Connell being close by, headed home. Shortly afterwards, Christmas nearly equalised, but the ball passed just over Watt's head.

   After the change of ends the play continued to be pretty even. Barbour completely beat Swepstone with a fast shot but the ball hit one of the posts and rebounded into play. Danskin smartly cleared an excellent shot by Radford, but unfortunately the ball only reached Prior, and a fast low shot by him was blocked by one of the Arsenal men in the mouth of the goal. The ball appeared to go over the cross-bar, but a goal was claimed and was allowed by the referee, in spite of a strong protest by the Arsenal men. For Clapton, Watts, Smith, Clark and Radford were the best of the backs, and Hayward did good work, while Connell and Parker were far and away the best among the forwards. The Arsenal team did not play to their best form, and they were not as strong as usual at halfback. Connolly, McBean, Howitt, Christmas, 'Edwards' and Barbour were the pick, but Robertson was not at his best.
*Teams:*
**Clapton:** H A Swepstone, goal; E J Watts and O O Hayward, backs; S Smith, T. Radford and R H Clark, halfbacks; J Sellar and G A Parker, right wing; W G Connell, centre, J S L Prior and J Bryson, left wing forwards.
**Royal Arsenal:** D Danskin, goal; P Connolly and J McBean, backs; D Howat, T Denham and W Stewart, halfbacks; A Christmas and C 'Edwards' right wing; H Barbour, centre; H R Robertson and H Offer, left wing forwards.

Two days later, Royal Arsenal played Mr W H Loraine's eleven, which included Billy Fry, the Caledonian player who sometimes turned out for the Arsenal. The game was played on a Monday, which was a general holiday for the Woolwich Arsenal due to annual stock-taking. The pitch was in good condition and the weather beautiful, with a crowd of 3,000.

**Royal Arsenal v Mr W H Loraine's Eleven, 31 March 1890**
From a scrummage in front of goal, five minutes before half-time, Barbour quickly headed the ball scoring the first goal for the Arsenal. Early into the second half Barraclough, with a bend shot, equalized. Barbour once again scored for the Arsenal with an accurate straight shot, which Seton failed to stop. Howat scored a third. Arsenal was not at full strength, but managed to win the fixture by 3–1.
*Team:*
**Royal Arsenal:** F W Beardsley, goal; P Connolly and J McBean, backs; W George, J M Bates and W Stewart, halfbacks; A Christmas and D Howat, right wing; H Barbour, centre, H Robertson and D Gloak, left wing forwards.

Arsenal's next eagerly anticipated game was against their old adversaries Old Westminsters for the London Charity Cup on 5 April. Moon, to their relief, was not in goal for the opposition because he had been selected to play for England against Scotland, but Old Westminsters fielded R R Sandilands, a speedy outside left, thought by many to be the best footballer produced by Westminster School. He later played for England.

The Arsenal also had a change inasmuch as the centre forward was a certain 'W C Edwards' who of course everyone knew was really the Scot Billy Fry. Using a pseudonym was quite common. The famous Welsh team The Druids had a forward named K Crosse. He had difficulty in getting time off for work, so used the name K Smith.

The London Charity Cup Final was decided at Leyton and attracted 8,000 spectators. This was by far the largest crowd at the Essex County Ground that season.

**Royal Arsenal v Old Westminsters, 5 April 1890**
Owing to the late arrival of some of the old boys, the start was not made until 3.48, when Barbour kicked off for the Arsenal. The Reds began in a determined manner. Only four minutes after the start a shot by Roberston at the Old Westminsters goal was followed in by

'Edwards' who scored the first goal. Even play followed, but again the Reds pressed forward, Edwards put through an accurate cross, and a second goal was scored by Christmas 12 minutes from the kick-off. The Old Boys spasmodically attacked, and a good shot by Sandilands forced Beardsley to use his hands. The Arsenal continued to take possession of the ball, and Offer beat Grant-Wilson with a long shot and scored the third goal. Just before the interval, Veitch moved into a dangerous position but he was quickly tackled by one of the backs.

After the change of ends the Old Boys showed more of their true form, and for nearly 30 minutes they had the best of the play. Street had a good chance but shot wide, and Woodbridge then kicked a shot over the bar. Veitch had a clear opening after some close play in front of the Arsenal goal, but he missed his chance. Probyn connected to the ball as it crossed in front of goal and scored. Encouraged by this success the Old Boys pushed forward, and in stopping a dangerous move, Connolly nearly scored against his side, the ball striking the inside of one of the side posts. The Old Boys were unable to score again, and towards the close the Arsenal once more took control of the game. The result: Arsenal 3, Old Westminsters 1.

For the visitors, the backs and halfbacks played a powerful game, but there was room for improvement in the passing of the forwards, 'Edwards', Barbour and Christmas doing the best work. The backs and the halfbacks on the other side worked hard, and the forwards passed well, but at times were a little ponderous. The play was fast, and the game was well contested.

*Teams:*

**Royal Arsenal:** F W Beardsley, goal; P Connolly and J M McBean, backs; D Howat, J M Bates (captain) and J W Julian, halfbacks; A Christmas and H Offer, right wing; H Barbour, centre; 'W C Edwards' and H R Robertson, left wing forwards.

**Old Westminsters:** C W Grant-Wilson, goal; C J Fox and R T Squire, backs; H Wetton, W Winckworth and H Harrison, halfbacks; P C Probyn and A R Woodbridge, right wing; J G Veitch, centre, F Street and R Sandilands, left wing forwards.

Umpires: F J Wall and R E Hetherington. Referee: F Barnett (Vice-President, London FA).

For David Danskin, what made it a perfect day was the combination of winning this game and the fact that Scotland put three goals past Moon to beat England 3–2 at The Oval.

One of the most popular facilities for the people of Woolwich was the Free Ferry, which caught fire again in May. It was built of pitch pine, a wood chosen for its self-preservative qualities but also very inflammable, and found to be difficult to extinguish once on fire. From the *Kentish Mercury*, 30 May 1890:

### The Woolwich Free Ferry on Fire

*At three minutes to twelve on Saturday noon the fire alarm at Market Hill suddenly rang at the Sun Street Fire Brigade Station. The engine was horsed and manned in one minute, and two more minutes sufficed for the firemen to reach the scene of conflagration. On their arrival they found 80 feet of the East Bridge in flames. Captain Young, in command of the ferryboat, had stopped the traffic and dispatched the crew to work the hose and hydrant kept available at the ferry. They kept a good supply of water on the top of the bridge whilst the brigade firemen worked their hose from the shore and from a boat, so as to reach the flames underneath. Both the boat's crew and the brigade firemen had the same employer, viz., the London County Council, and they worked with great energy and heartiness for fifteen minutes, when the fire was declared to be out. During the short time it had been burning a vast amount of damage had been done. The bridge is constructed of very thick planks 8 ft long, laid down crossways and rested on iron girders. A very strong sun had heated the pitch and the planks were in a favourable condition for catching fire and a lighted match or tobacco thoughtlessly thrown down by some passenger had doubtless set the pier in flames. After the fire was put out a careful examination was made to determine as to whether the footbridge was safe for passengers. It was found that 80-foot lengths had been considerably charred and weakened by the fire, and would have to be replaced by new sleepers; but the planks were found to be strong enough to stand the foot traffic, that was resumed in the afternoon. The engines from Shooters Hill, Blackheath and Greenwich arrived with incredible speed, and the public may be assured that the fire extinguishing arrangements in the Woolwich district are as near perfection as possible. Had they been otherwise, the new Free Ferry would have been doomed. It was, as the firemen call it, 'a good stop'. Whilst the Woolwich Ferry was on fire the Southend Pier, so well known to Woolwichers, was in flames. The hot sun heated the pitch as at Woolwich, and rendered the wood favourable for taking fire, 50 ft of the old portion of the pier being destroyed. The fine new pier at Liverpool was burned down under similar circumstances.*

Fortunately during the fracas nobody fell in the river. Some parts were bad and some parts were just terrible, it depended on where you were. Naturally the worst parts were the sewer outfalls. Incredibly people still swam in the foul water and some drowned.

In the summer, Hope Robertson signed for his new club Everton. He was later that year to marry a Liverpool girl, Elizabeth Phipps. In the 1890–1 season he only made a few first-team appearances (Everton were Football League champions that year), but in the 1891–2 season he was a first team regular. Later he was to move to Bootle and then Walsall Town Swifts. When his football career was over he returned to his old trade in shipbuilding.

**Six-a-side competition, 30 May 1890**
Royal Arsenal entered a team for the six-a-side competition at the Agricultural Hall, London. The competition continued over two nights and was based on a points system, ten points for a goal and five for a corner, with one point being deducted from any team that kicked the ball out of play. Arsenal (captained by Bill Julian) won the final against the Caledonians 1–0. As usual Albert Christmas scored most of the goals, including the one in the final. The teams were honoured by the presence of the Prince of Wales each evening. Albert appeared in five trophy-winning sides that season.

By the beginning of June 1890, the Torpedo Factory had been handed over to the Royal Gun Factory. About 400 hands went with the transfer. The change was made to equalize the departments.

A considerable number of Arsenal workmen, chiefly in the Royal Laboratory, were stood out through slackness of work, mainly through want of materials, and it was hoped to be only for a temporary period. The Parliamentary grant to the Arsenal that year was larger than the previous year, and workers felt that as long as private companies did not succeed in getting work away from Woolwich, there was no reason to think that work at the Arsenal would be reduced on a permanent basis. They felt that mismanagement had contributed to the situation.

The Scottish League was formed in 1890, in time for the 1890–1 season. Eleven clubs joined: Abercorn, Cambuslang, Celtic, Cowlairs, Dumbarton, Hearts, Rangers, Renton, St Mirren, Third Lanark and Vale of Leven. It was not long, however, before the Scottish League was torn apart by the same dispute that had nearly split the game in England – paying players. Renton had played only five matches when they were expelled from the league for playing Edinburgh Saints, a team that the Scottish FA decided was professional. The Scots were even more determined than the English to keep their game 'pure' and amateur.

On 6 September Arsenal commenced the new football season at the Invicta Recreation Ground, Plumstead. The grounds were now multi-purpose, and a cycle track ran round the outside of the football pitch. A popular cycle fixture could attract an attendance of over 10,000. Fortunately cycle meetings were normally held on a Sunday. So far as the Arsenal players were concerned, the best facility was the provision of purpose-built changing rooms, a vast improvement over the disused railway wagon they had used at the Manor Field.

From the *Kentish Mercury*, 12 September 1890:

> *Some few years back, the idea was mooted as to the formation of a football club in connection with the Royal Arsenal, and the adoption of the Association Rules. The suggestion was met with ridicule and prediction of certain failure, but how entirely erroneous these surmises were was proved wrong by the enormous assembly at the opening of the 1890/91 season, on Saturday. For the first two or three seasons the 'Reds' were always classed under the heading of 'medium' strength, but, being managed by an energetic committee, and supported by that influence which the Arsenal is sure to command, the club has now grown to be one of the most formidable of those playing under the dribbling code in the south of England. Whereas at the commencement of their career the average 'gate' was about 500, that number during the past two seasons has developed to more like 5,000, and after their success of last year it was not surprising to find a larger*

*gathering on Saturday, when close upon 8,000 were present. The small charge (3d) for admission may have a great deal to do with the popularity of the game in the district but, be that as it may, it can confidently be said that in no other part of the Metropolis is the interest in Association football so great as at Plumstead.*

*The inauguration of the ensuing season was the occasion of the opening of the club's new grounds – the Invicta Recreation Grounds – in the High Street, Plumstead, and when completed will be one of the finest football grounds in the south. The grandstand, which will accommodate about 1,500, was draped on Saturday with red cloth, decorated with trophies of flags, whilst streamers were hung from the flagstaff in the centre to the end of the building, and presented in very gay appearance. The weather, which during the forenoon had been overcast and oppressive, became extremely fine, and the sun, shining with mid-summer like strength, raised the temperature to a degree more suited for cricket than the winter pastime. Long before the hour appointed for the commencement of the game hundreds were to be seen wending their way towards the entrance in the High Street, and by 3.15 every available place from which a good view of the game could be obtained was taken advantage of, the stand and the terrace being packed. Whilst the spectators were flocking into the ground the band of the 2nd Kent Artillery Volunteers, under the direction of Sergeant-Major Little, played a capital selection of music, and also during the interval at half time; and at the conclusion of the match they performed for about an hour. For the opening fixture the 93rd Highlanders (from Bisley) were encountered, and being the winners of the Army Cup of 1888/89, the expectations as to a close contest were fully realised.*

Offer was not available for the first match so Pell, who had played in the previous season's reserves, took his place on the left wing. Edmund Bee, a goalkeeper, was to make his debut. Edmund was born in Nottingham in 1868 and he was 5 ft 8 in tall and weighed 11 stone. He had played for various clubs in Nottingham; and by trade was a bricklayer. 'Time waits for no man', and it was appropriate that Fred

Beardsley was to be replaced by a Nottingham man. Fred continued to play for the reserves. His age then was 34. Also making his debut was William Campbell from Inverness.

**Royal Arsenal v 93rd Highlanders, 6 September 1890**

At 3.30 the home team entered the field, and were greeted by loud applause, which was repeated some five minutes later on the appearance of the Highlanders. Winning the toss, the Highlanders elected to play with the sun at their back, and at a quarter to four the Reds kicked off.

Thomson quickly intercepted the ball, and passed to Fleming who was tackled by Bates and he, in turn, kicked the ball deep into the Highlanders half. The Reds pressed for some time, and Robertson was called upon make several saves. Roy dribbled the ball to the centre of the field and a short period of even play followed. The Reds then returned to the attack, led by Christmas, Barbour and Pell. Christmas sent in a long shot from the wing that Robertson was just able to save. The Highlanders attacked in numbers, and Young, taking a good pass from Roy, sent in an excellent shot that Bee fisted out. Julian and Christmas took the ball into their opponents' half, and from a pass from Christmas, Barbour had a clear shot on goal, but it lacked power and was easily saved by Robertson. Shortly afterwards Christmas sent in another long shot from the wing, which Kedens kicked away. Once more the Reds attacked, and from a scrummage in front of the Highlanders' goal, Gloak sent in a lofted shot, which Robertson was unable to reach, and scored the initial goal of the season for the Reds, amidst loud cheering.

This made the Highlanders more determined, and on restarting, the game was switched from one end of the field to the other. 'Hands' to the Reds was followed by a couple of corners, which were unproductive. McLafferty put in an excellent dribble, to take the ball to the Reds' goal and it appeared that the Highlanders would score, but Bee, rushing in, kicked the ball away amidst loud applause. The Highlanders then took possession and forced a corner off Howat, but the ball went into touch. Some brilliant passing and dribbling by Roy, McLafferty and Fleming received loud applause, but Connolly tackled Fleming, and made a good clearance. A free kick was given against the Reds for a foul to no effect. Stirratt and Thomson then combined well, and from a centre by Roy, Young almost scored, the ball just passing wide of the post. A foul against the Reds close to their goal was not productive. Similarly, a foul against the Highlanders soon after produced the same result. Connolly headed away a well-placed shot by Stirratt, whilst shortly afterwards Campbell, taking a long kick from Connolly, made a fine shot at goal that only just missed. Some excellent passing by Roy and McLafferty followed, and Denholm passed to Fleming, who kicked into touch. 'Hands' was given against the Reds close to their goal but McBean headed the ball away. The Reds attacked again. Christmas passed the ball to Howat, who had an opportunity to score, but skimmed over the cross-bar. Several unproductive 'scrummages' took place near the Reds' goal, and half-time arrived with the score 1–0 in favour of the Reds.

The Highlanders resumed the initiative at the beginning of the second half, and McLafferty sent in a shot that struck the post and went into touch. Barbour cleared; Roy picked up a loose ball and centred to McLafferty, who once more sent in a stinging shot, well saved by Bee. At this point the Reds appeared to tire, and the Highlanders took control of the game. The Arsenal goalkeeper was called upon to save some hot shots, but at last Roy sent in a high one, which Bee was unable to reach, to make the score 1–1. The game was then stopped for a few minutes because Howat had been seized with cramp. Good dribbling and inter-passing by Christmas, Barbour and Pell took the ball into the opposition's area, and the Reds looked as if they were certain to score. However, the visitors' goal was not in danger long, as Fleming and McLafferty took the ball well into the Arsenal half. Julian then put in a good dribble, but was tackled by Turner, who centred to McMillan, whose shot went wide. By the aid of Campbell and Barbour, the Reds almost scored. Their efforts were thwarted by McLafferty's long clearance. The Highlanders kept up the pressure until the finish, with Roy, McLafferty and Fleming sending in some stinging shots. Bee made some fine saves and no further goals were scored. The game ended in a 1–1 draw.

*Teams:*

**Royal Arsenal:** E Bee, goal; P Connolly and J McBean, backs; D Howat, J Bates (captain) and J W Julian, halfbacks; A Christmas, W Campbell, H Barbour, D Gloak and T Pell, forwards.

**93<sup>rd</sup> Highlanders:** T Robertson, goal; J Stirratt and I Kedens (captain), backs; A Thomson, J McMillan and J Turner, halfbacks; J Roy, J Denholm, C McLafferty, Young and J Fleming, forwards.

After the match the visitors were entertained by the Reds to high tea in the Committee Room under the stand. Mr Davis (Chairman of the

Committee) presided, and a pleasant evening was interspersed with short speeches, the health of the opposing team being received with loud applause.

On 14 September Arsenal played a friendly match against the Casuals, a team of gentlemen players who at this time included J G Veitch (Old Westminsters and later England international), C W G Wilson (Oxford University and England), W A Winckworth (Old Westminsters and later England), R R Barker (Casuals and England), A H Harrison (Old Westminsters and England), R R Sandilands (Old Westminster and England), and of course, C B Fry.

Charles Burgess Fry was educated at Repton School and Oxford University, where he excelled in Association and Rugby Union football. For four years he gave sterling service to Oxford, captained the Association team in his final year, and was always a sound and reliable fullback. He also represented Oxford at rugby. He later played as one of the Blackheath three-quarters.

Fry made football appearances for England against Canada in 1891, against Ireland in 1901 and for Southampton against Sheffield United in the Cup Final of 1902. His footballing accomplishments were small compared with his achievements in cricket and athletics. He held the record for the amateur long jump and ran for Oxford in the 100 yards. In 1894 he scored a captain's century. In 1912 at the age of 40 he led England to success against both Australia and South Africa in the Triangular Tournament. At the age of 49 he was invited to captain England against Warwick Armstrong's Australians, but declined because of injury.

### Royal Arsenal v Casuals, 14 September 1890

Fine weather favoured this encounter in September at the Invicta Recreation Grounds, Plumstead, when some 7,000 assembled to witness the struggle for supremacy between the above teams.

The Reds won the toss and elected to play from the entrance end, and Veitch kicked off for the visitors. The Casuals had the best of the early play. Then from a neat pass by Veitch, Sandilands scored the first goal. From the Reds' kick-off the play moved into the Casuals' goal area, and Christmas tried hard to score, but was tackled by Wilson. Some exciting play followed, and a corner to the Casuals was unsuccessful, but soon after Veitch and Cox put in a fine combined dribble. Cox then passed to Sandilands, who took a quick shot at goal which beat Bee, scoring the second goal for the visitors, 0–2. Sandilands next sent in a powerful shot that Bee did well to save. Offer dribbled down the field, but retained possession too long, and Pares cleared. The Reds again pressed, and Christmas centred to Barbour, who made an excellent shot. Although the ball appeared to go through the posts no goal was allowed.

Play was even for a short time when Campbell, receiving the ball from McBean, made a fine run right through, and when close to the goal, passed to Offer (who was palpably offside), and centred to Christmas who shot through the posts, but the goal was disallowed. The Reds then attacked strongly. From a corner to the Reds, Barbour sent in a stinging shot that beat Wilson, and scored the first goal for the Arsenal, 1–2. Immediately afterwards Christmas, receiving the ball from Howat, scored a second goal for the Reds amidst great enthusiasm to make it 2–2. On restarting 'hands' was given against the Reds. Winckworth took the kick, and passed the ball to Nixon, who sent in a low shot that beat Bee. The score at half-time: Casuals 3, Arsenal 2.

After half-time Wilson was injured and substituted by Brandon in goal. Barbour restarted the game. The Reds attacked, pushing the ball into the Casuals' half. Harrison attempted to clear but miskicked, which gave Campbell an opening from which he equalized, 3–3. Barbour was then prominent with a long dribble, and made a neat pass to Christmas who scored another goal, 4–3. Barbour carried the ball well into the Casuals' territory, and Julian had an unproductive shot. Gloak, Offer and Campbell were then prominent, and from a scrummage round the visitor's goal, Gloak had an opening but sent the ball high over the cross-bar. Fry kicked out, and Campbell took possession, and then made a long dribble towards the goal and scored the fifth goal for the Reds, 5–3.

The Casuals took the initiative and the ball was taken into the Reds' half. Both Veitch and Sandilands hit shots that Bee fisted out. Christmas dribbled well and passed to Offer, who in turn passed to Gloak, who shot into touch. The Casuals were again penalized for 'hands', but Veitch quickly collected a loose ball, and some neat passing followed between Cox, Veitch and Sandilands, close to the Reds' goal. Then Sandilands beat Bee with a vicious shot, and scored the fourth goal for the Casuals. The Reds still continued to press, and, from a pass by Gloak, Christmas nearly scored, the ball just missing the post. For the last five minutes the Casuals backs were kept under immense pressure, Campbell and Christmas several times nearly scoring. Nothing further was scored, and a splendid game ended in a well-earned victory for the Reds 5–4.

*Teams:*

**Royal Arsenal:** E Bee, goal; P Connolly and J McBean, backs; D Howat, W S Stewart and J W Julian (captain), halfbacks; A Christmas and W C Campbell, right wing, H Barbour, centre, H Offer and D Gloak, left wing forwards.

**Casuals:** C W G Wilson, goal; C B Fry and A H Harrison, backs; W W Winckworth, R R Barker and B Pares, halfbacks; H C Barraclough and A C Nixon (captain), right wing, J G Veitch, centre, R R Sandilands and L L Cox, left wing forwards.

Referee: A G O Kennedy (Hon Sec, Kent County Football Association). Umpires: W B Jackson (Royal Arsenal) and T W Blenkiron (Old Carthusians).

Unfortunately the team were all getting older, and Morris Bates was no exception. On the same day that the first team were playing the Casuals, Morris was captain of the Reserves, who were playing Millwall Athletic away. In the first half Arsenal was able to contain the Millwall forward line, but in the second half with the wind behind them Millwall ran amok. They won the game 4–0.

**Royal Arsenal Reserves v Cray Wanderers, 4 October 1890**

The reserves were to win this match by 2–0, with the goals scored by Simonds and Grandison. This game is only significant because in the first half Richard Horsington was again injured, and the team was forced to continue with ten men. This injury ended Richard's fine football career. Fortunately he had a good business brain and his future was secure.

# Chapter 5

One very sad event was James Charteris breaking his leg in two places, in a game that should never have taken place because of the atrocious weather conditions. The serious injury sustained that day finished his playing career. His drive and scoring ability were much missed by the Reds. From the *Kentish Mercury*, 5 December 1890:

*Serious Accident to a Player*

*The Royal Arsenal Football Club had two matches down for decision at Plumstead, on Monday, 26th November, one versus Boston (Lincolnshire), at the Invicta Recreation Grounds, and the other (a Kent County Senior Cup Tie) with Beckenham on the Manor Field. It having been announced up till the last moment that the matches would take place, several thousands made their way to the grounds, and great was the disappointment when it was found that both had been abandoned. As it was found impossible to clear the snow from the Manor Field, it was decided, at a meeting held on Friday night, to scratch the first named match and play the Cup Tie on the Invicta grounds, the 'Reds' Secretary wiring to the Secretary of the Beckenham Club to that effect. In reply a telegram was received from the last named official at a quarter to one on Saturday, stating that, owing to the state of the weather, the Beckenham team would not play, although two of the teams, we are informed were actually on the ground at the time appointed for the game. Several messages were then exchanged, the Secretary of the home team contending that the ground was playable, his opinion being upheld by that of the referee Mr H. Pickett (Essex County FC), and a final telegram was dispatched by the home Secretary to the effect that, in the event of non-appearance of the Beckenham team, they would claim the tie. Several thousands having passed the turnstiles and no team arriving, it was decided that with the help of some players belonging to the White Hart (another local club) to play a scratch game, the sides being chosen by J.M. Bates and W. George. The game had only been in progress a quarter of an hour when Campbell came into collision with Charteris, and the latter, in trying to get the ball away, slipped, and falling with his leg under him broke it in two places below the knee. Dr. Coleman, who was on the ground, attended to the sufferer, and he was afterwards conveyed to the Plumstead Infirmary. Charteris we are glad to learn is progressing satisfactorily.*

In December the Arsenal played Cambridge University at the Invicta Ground, with an attendance of approximately 6,500. The snow had been swept off the ground and the thaw had set in, so conditions were good. Arsenal had the assistance of the Caledonian player Billy Fry.

Cambridge's best player was M H (Hugh) Stanbrough, a 'flying outside left', who had plenty of pace and ball control. Hugh also played for the Old Carthusians and the Corinthians. He was later to be selected for the England Amateur Eleven. Their goalkeeper Gay was a first class cricketer who was to play for England. Cambridge played in their normal light blue and white halved shirts.

**Royal Arsenal v Cambridge University, 1 December 1890**
Campbell scored the first goal with a low bending shot just before half-time. After the resumption, following a neat dribble Barbour passed the ball to Offer, who scored the second goal. The pace of the Arsenal team was beginning to tell, but against the run of play, Dewhurst scored with a high cross shot for Cambridge. From then on the Arsenal dominated the match, adding another three goals by Campbell, Fry and Barbour to win 5–1.
*Teams:*
**Arsenal:** E Bee, goal; P Connolly and J McBean, backs; D Howat, W S Stewart and J W Julian, halfbacks; A Christmas and W C Campbell, right wing; H Barbour (captain), centre, W E Fry and H Offer, left wing forwards.
**Cambridge University:** L H Gay, goal; F J Kittermaster and J R Panli, backs; W K Fernie, N C Cooper and F C Streatfield, halfbacks; W F H Stanborough and G P Dewhurst, right wing; P Shaw, centre; M H Stanborough and Llewellyn-Davies, left wing forwards.
Umpires: A Singleton (Royal Arsenal FC) and E F Halstead (Cambridge University FC). Referee: N L Jackson (Corinthians FC).

Mr N L Jackson, known as 'Pa' Jackson, was a first-class manager and organizer. He was the founder of the Corinthians and numerous golf clubs.

In 1891 many innovations were introduced. Umpires were replaced by referees and linesmen, referees were allowed on the field of play with whistles and notebooks, the penalty kick was introduced, Arsenal turned professional and changed their name to the Woolwich Arsenal, and Mr J A Brodie, a Liverpool city engineer, was credited with inventing football nets. These were officially introduced in a trial match between north and south in Nottingham. They proved very popular and were soon in use on a regular basis.

In January disaster struck David Danskin's brother-in-law Nick. He ran a small dairy in New Cross Road. The premises consisted of a shop that was split into two, and Nick had taken one half, on a three-year lease. One morning he found that the landlord had turned off his water supply. While Nick was occasionally late in paying the rent, this did not, in David's view, justify cutting off his water supply. It later transpired that the landlord had received a better offer for the lease of

A retired Albert Christmas

the whole shop, and eventually Nick vacated the premises after receiving a small amount of compensation. This was the end of his dairy business, but being a very able bookkeeper, he soon obtained a suitable job. Of course, like the Fletchers, he would have preferred to work for himself, but it was not practical for him to do so.

It was fortunate that the Fletchers' bakery business was successful, and the premises large, as there were now six sons to feed: George, Ralph, Jonathan, Ebenezer, Nicholas and Herbert. On the second floor there were seven bedrooms, and the first floor had a good-size front room with two large back rooms. The ground floor comprised a large shop with a small parlour, a kitchen with a large scullery, and WC. To the rear was a bakehouse with a part-glazed roof. There was a brick-built four-stall stable and loose box together with a wooden three-stall stable in the yard. The property was leasehold with a rent of approximately £50 per annum. It was a lively house with three assistants living in.

At long last the local authorities were taking action against slum landlords in the Greenwich and Woolwich areas. In 1890 the Housing of the Working Classes Act became law. This gave to the local Board of Works the power to close unsanitary houses, and allowed them to build council houses.

In January 1891 summonses were issued to a number of slum property landlords, including Joseph Francis Swann, the owner of numerous properties in Morley Road and Lombard Road, Greenwich. The main complaints were that the majority of the properties had defective water supplies to the closets. In Morley Road the sewerage matter from the houses was discharged into a cesspool in a nearby field. This in turn overflowed into a ditch. This was the first step towards slum clearance.

On Saturday 3 January the Royal Arsenal Reserves played the Polytechnic at the Invicta Ground, which resulted in a 4–1 win for the Arsenal. Two of the Arsenal players were of interest, F W Beardsley in goal and P Connolly on the right wing, and a certain W George played for the Polytechnic.

There were many controversial issues to be discussed at the club's Annual General Meeting on Tuesday 6 January 1891. From the *Kentish Mercury*, 9 January 1891:

> ### Royal Arsenal Football Club AGM
> *A general meeting of members was held on Tuesday at the hall adjoining the Windsor Castle, Maxey Road, Plum-*

stead, Mr Davis presided. There was a large attendance. The Hon. Sec. (Mr G. H. Osbourne) reported that to the present date the first team had played 15 matches, won 11, drawn 3, and lost 1. The goals for the club were 45, average of 3, against 14, average of 1. The first team's opponents had scored 4 goals once, 3 twice and 1 on 6 occasions. The second team had played 14 matches not including those down for Christmas week, and had won 12, drawn 1 and lost 1. The second team's opponents had scored 4 twice, 1 on four occasions and eight times had failed to score. In the Charity Cup Competition they were to play the Crusaders on February 14$^{th}$. The committee had decided to give the gate for this match to the Charity. The Club had been asked to play for the Dartford and District Cup, and the Rochester and District Cup but had declined. For November 1891, they have arranged a match with the Canadians.

Mr Humble in answer to Mr Turner, said that in the only match lost, in which he acted as umpire, he gave a goal against the Arsenal Club because he honestly believed that the ball did not go within two feet of reaching between the posts. He would rather have his right hand cut off than getting a victory by the Arsenal by unfair terms.

Mr Singleton said they had had a great deal of trouble about the Senior Kent Cup, and he moved that the Club withdraw from the competition. He thought it would be very much to the monetary advantage of the club to drop this competition as they had very few Saturdays to spare, and further the Association had treated them very shabbily over the match at Gravesend last year, and that against Beckenham this season (cheers).

Mr Wells seconded.

Mr Beardsley moved an amendment that the club adhered to the arrangements for the second team to play in this Competition, the second team being strengthened if necessary.

The amendment was carried.

Captain McCanlie and Mr Greenwood were elected Auditors and Mr Turner, provisional Auditor.

Several notices of motion were given, including one

*from Mr Peplow to pay the Secretary. The Chairman announced, amidst cheers that Offer had been invited to play for the South against North.*

*Mr Singleton indignantly repudiated any part in getting Campbell to join Preston North End.*

*The proceedings closed with thanks to the Chairman.*

Mr Singleton's remarks regarding the Senior Kent Cup referred to the game when Arsenal refused to play extra time against Gravesend in a Kent Senior Cup-tie. They were subsequently disqualified. Beckenham were right in withdrawing due to bad conditions. Charteris subsequently broke his leg in the substitute scratch game.

There was much unrest about the signing of William Campbell as a professional by Preston North End. Campbell was an extrovert and a crowd pleaser but a thorn in the side of any management. Some were suspicious where Preston-born Alfred Singleton's loyalties lay. Campbell left under the impression that he had a long-term contract with the Invincibles.

Preston North End was beginning by their standards to go through a bad patch. Basically Campbell had been brought in to replace England international John Goodall, but their expectations were too high because Campbell was an enthusiastic novice. Preston's other problem was that their squad was one of the smallest in the English League. They relied heavily on their long-serving existing players, including the brilliant Nick Ross, former captain of Heart of Midlothian, who could play either as a fullback or forward, his brother Jimmy Ross, a very successful forward, and James Trainer, known as the 'Prince of Goalkeepers'. He played as a Welsh international 16 times, and would have played more but for the demands of Preston North End.

By February 1891 Preston North End decided to dispense with Campbell's services. David Russell from Hearts, who from their point of view was equally disastrous, replaced him. Russell was to have the last laugh. He was transferred back to Hearts who tried him in the centre half position, which was highly successful, and he was picked to play for Scotland.

Meanwhile Campbell had been briefly transferred to Middlesbrough, who failed to appreciate his demands. Campbell's next club in 1892–3 was second division Darwen, where he was a successful regular, but at the end of the season he was suspended by the FA for a misdemeanour. Blackburn Rovers had been impressed by his skilful soccer performances with Darwen, and duly signed him, but his reappearance was delayed due to his suspension until October. Blackburn was not impressed with his debut. He was unfit and lacklustre, and they dispensed with his services in November 1893. He then signed for Newton Heath (Manchester United), which was one of the weaker sides in the first division. The team was nicknamed 'The Heathens' and they had a very rough reputation. Three of their players, Perrins, Donaldson and Clements, were suspended following a game at Derby. In a later match against West Bromwich Albion, the local Birmingham newspaper accused the Newton Heath team of brutality. Campbell's stay was again brief, playing five games, and scoring one goal.

In February 1894 he joined Notts County, then in Division Two. In May 1894 he was suspended for two years by the Football League for making an illegal approach for John Murray of Blackburn on behalf of Notts County. For two seasons Campbell played in non-league football. In 1896–7 a certain W C Campbell played three matches for Everton, scoring one goal.

In January 1891 Arsenal was to face a hard test. Their opponents were Derby County in the first round of the FA Cup. Derby was of course one of the founder members of the football league. Derby County's star player was Johnny Goodall, their captain, who had formerly played for Preston North End. He was also a good all-round cricketer and played for Derbyshire. There was an attendance of approximately 9,000 at the Invicta Recreation Ground for this Cup-tie.

### Royal Arsenal v Derby County, 17 January 1891

The sun was shining brightly but there was a keen frosty air. The ground was in an appalling condition and but for the downfall of snow late in the morning, it is doubtful whether the game could have been decided, as it would have been very dangerous to play on the ice-covered surface. The centre had been covered with sand, but throughout the game the men found the going terribly heavy and falls were frequent.

Derby started well and by half-time was leading by 2–1, the Reds' goal deservedly scored by Offer, whose dextrous play was outstanding. Many attacks were made on the Derby goal, but the Reds lacked sharpness when positioned to score.

In the second half the Reds' play improved, and for a period of about 20 minutes they kept up a fierce onslaught on the visitors' goal, but failed to score. The Derby goalkeeper Bunyan made some fantastic saves. The crowd enjoyed an exciting match. Derby's clever short passing was especially appreciated. Offer was the best of the Arsenal forwards. Gloak, Christmas and Meggs worked hard, Bee was as sharp as usual. The backs played well, but Barbour was disappointing. No further goals were scored. Derby won the tie 2–1.

*Teams:*

**Royal Arsenal:** E Bee, goal; P Connolly and J McBean, backs; D Howat, W S Stewart, and J W Julian, halfbacks: J Meggs and A Christmas, right wing, H Barbour (captain), centre, and H Offer and D Gloak, left wing forwards.

**Derby County:** Bunyan, goal; Baker and A Goodall, backs; Walker, Chalmers and Roulstone, halfbacks; Bakewell and McLachlan, right wing, John Goodall (captain), centre, Cooper and McMillan, left wing forwards.

Umpires: F E Saunders and S R Carr. Referee: N L Jackson.

Johnny Goodall continued to be selected for England until 1898. He was always proud of his personal fitness. He continued playing until 1913, at the age of 49, when he was manager of the Southern League, Division II Welsh side Mardy.

That season Arsenal reached the final of the London Cup. Their opponents were St Bartholomew's, and the venue was Kennington Oval.

St Barts' star players were F E Fernie (one of the Swifts team that had beaten Arsenal in the FA Cup in December 1889); J F Fernie, a former student at Wellingborough Grammar School who played for the Casuals and the Crusaders (and later became a member of the Corinthians), and G A Coulby, the St Barts goalkeeper, who had also played for the Crusaders against Arsenal.

There had been heavy rain that morning, which left the turf a little slippery, but it did not affect the game to any great extent. The attendance was approximately 5,500. The majority of the crowd was wearing Arsenal's red rosettes.

**Royal Arsenal v St Bartholomew's, 7 March 1891**

The Medicos arrived first some minutes in advance of the Reds, the appearance of the latter being the signal for tremendous cheering. The Reds won the toss, and commenced from the Vauxhall end. After some mixed play Christmas at last broke away and finished a neat run with a good shot, the ball just skimming the upright. The Reds attacked in force, and from a neat pass by Christmas, Offer sent the ball past Coulby and scored the first goal. Arsenal again pressed, and Barbour finished an excellent dribble by scoring the second goal for the Reds. The Reds' class was now beginning to tell. Connolly added the third goal. The Reds were positive, Connolly scored the fourth goal from a long shot, and immediately after from a neat cross from Barbour, Gloak scored the fifth goal. The half-time score was 5–0.

Barbour kicked off for the Reds. It was apparent that the Arsenal team considered the game won, and they did not attack with the same fervour, although the Medicos did attempt to compete. Nearing the end, Fry, with a long side shot, scored the sixth goal for the Reds. The Medicos made a final determined effort but the final score was 6–0 to Arsenal.

*Teams:*

**Royal Arsenal:** E Bee, goal; P Connolly and J McBean, backs; D Howat, W S Stewart and J W Julian (captain), halfbacks; A Christmas and H Offer, right wing, H Barbour, centre, D Gloak and W E Fry, left wing forwards.

**St Bartholomews Hospital:** G A Coulby, goal; J S Mackintosh and F E Fernie, backs; F Lewarnie, J G Faber and E Henry, halfbacks; R G Hogarth (captain) and W E Bond, left wing, F J Dixon, centre, N O Wilson and J F Fernie, right wing forwards.

Umpires: W H Harding (Hotspur) and W Crosier-Hayne (Old Cranleighhams). Referee T Gunning (Hon Sec London FA).

The *Kentish Mercury* reported on 3 April 1891:

> *Royal Arsenal Football Club Matches*
> 'The Invicta Recreation Grounds Plumstead – the ground of the now famous team as familiarly known as the 'Reds' which is without doubt the most popular ground on which Association Football is regularly played in the South of England – having drawn together such enormous crowds during the present season, it was fully expected that the mammoth programme put forward by the Arsenal Executive for the Easter holidays at that resort would prove a source of great attraction. Two matches were fixed for Good Friday, Saturday, and Easter Monday, and on Easter Tuesday one fixture was arranged, and when it was announced that the list comprised such teams as the Heart of Midlothian (winners of this year's Scottish Association Cup and the Edinburgh Challenge Shield), Nottingham Forest, Old*

*Harrovians, the Highland Light Infantry, City Ramblers, Crouch End, and the final tie between White Hart and Clarence for the Milton Challenge Shield, speculation was at once rife that record attendances would be the order of the day. Although those of the morning matches were not, with the exception, perhaps of the Milton Final, so large as might have been expected, averaging about 3,000, this number was fully atoned for by those of the afternoon, when the average must have been something like 10,000, for on Monday afternoon the crowd did not fall far short of 15,000. The Arsenal teams for the matches were rather a mixed lot, notable absentees from the ranks being McBean, Fry, and Offer, but several players made an exceedingly promising appearance in the first eleven viz., Croxen, Collins, Wood, Taylor and Johnstone.*

*Although the weather was bitterly cold Good Friday morning, some 3,000 persons were present to witness the match against City Ramblers. The Arsenal team for this game was a reserve side captained by Simmons, the one-armed player. The athlete 'Jack' Sheppard was one of the backs. The former Arsenal player Jimmy Meggs featured for City Ramblers.*

**Royal Arsenal v City Ramblers, 27 March 1891**
The Ramblers kicked off and initially the game went end to end. Parkinson scored for the home team with a long shot. Several corners and free kicks were then awarded to both teams, but neither was able to score, and at half-time the Reds were leading 1–0. Simmons restarted and after a fine run by Jimmy Meggs, he then passed to Whitehouse, who equalized within a minute from the restart. Simmons, Mace and Pell on one side, and brothers Meggs and Whitehouse on the other, were frequently prominent with some clever play, but nothing further was scored, and after an excellent contest the game ended in a 1–1 draw. Of the Arsenal team, Parkinson, Simmons and Mace were the pick; while of the visitors the brothers Meggs, Whitehouse, Ingram, and Thomas were the best, the latter's goalkeeping being outstanding.
*Teams:*
**Royal Arsenal:** Leaney, goal; Roe and Houghton, backs; Sheppard, Sandover and Parkinson, halfbacks; Pell and Halsy, right wing, Simmons (captain) centre, Russell and Mace, left wing forwards.

**City Ramblers:** Thomas, goal; Marsh and Boas, backs; Ingram, Merdin and Harris, halfbacks; G Meggs and J Meggs, right wing, Rambler, centre, Whitehouse and Brownleigh, left wing forwards.

The game against the Highlanders was played on Good Friday afternoon in front of 6,000 spectators.

**Royal Arsenal v the 71st Highland Light Infantry, 27 March 1891**

Barbour kicked off for the Reds, who immediately attacked, with Gloak on three occasions kicking the ball over the cross-bar. The military were awarded a free kick for 'hands' but failed to take advantage. A free kick was then awarded to Arsenal, which Galloway attempted to clear. The ball only reached Croxen, who passed neatly to Gloak, who scored the first goal for the Reds. The military then pressurized the Arsenal goal, but they were unable to break through the home team's defence. After a spell of even play Gloak and Christmas went clear, and Christmas scored with a good shot. The Reds attacked for some time. Christmas received a pass from Croxen and scored again for the Reds. The military fought back determinedly and Caldwell scored with a long shot, the result being 3–1 to the Arsenal.

*Team:*

**Royal Arsenal:** E Taylor, goal; P Connolly and W Collins, backs; D Howat, W S Stewart and J W Julian (captain) halfbacks; A Croxen and R Mills, right wing, H Barbour, centre, D Gloak and A Christmas, left wing forwards.

In the next game Arsenal played Heart of Midlothian, which included four Scottish internationals: J Adams, I Begbie, J Hill and D Baird. Hearts were known as the 'Jam tarts' or the 'Jammos'. This match proved to be the most attractive of the series, for on Easter Monday afternoon some 15,000 spectators were present to witness the encounter. The Heart of Midlothian team came with a splendid reputation, having proved successful in the final tie of the Scottish Challenge cup that season, and having also carried off the Edinburgh Shield.

**Royal Arsenal v Heart of Midlothian, 30 March 1891**

Barbour started the game, and the Reds immediately attacked. Johnstone shot wide. Smart play between Wood, Gloak and Johnstone confined play to the visitors' half until Russell put in a clever single-handed run and shot over. From the goal kick a corner fell to the visitors, which was cleared, as were four others they obtained in quick succession. For some time play was even, nearly every member of each team being frequently prominent. Wood then put in a fine dribble and crossed to Howat, who scored for the Reds amidst tremendous cheering. After this reverse the visitors fought back with great determination, and it was not long before Taylor equalized from a neat cross by Russell. The Reds then pressed, and when a score seemed inevitable from a shot by Wood, Fairbairn just managed to clear, so the teams crossed over with a score of 1–1.

Russell restarted, and after the Reds had attacked for some time, Russell dashed away and passed to Mason, who crossed to Baird and that player scored a second goal for the visitors. After a free kick had been awarded to the Reds and Barbour had headed over, Mason and Russell then led another onslaught on the home goal, and Baird and Mason quickly added two more goals, making the score 4–1 against the Reds. Good play between the forwards, led by Gloak and Wood, confined the ball to the Jammos' goal area for some while, then Hearts broke away and Hill scored their fifth goal. From then on the Reds crowded the visitors' goal, but despite some brilliant play on the part of Julian, Christmas, Wood and Johnstone, failed to score. Hearts were victorious 5–1.
*Team:*
**Royal Arsenal:** E Bee, goal; P Connolly and W Collins, backs; W S Stewart, Johnstone and J W Julian, halfbacks; A Christmas and D Howat, right wing, H Barbour, centre, D Gloak and Wood, right wing forwards.

The final match of the Easter programme was played on Tuesday 31 March against Nottingham Forest, who were playing the second match of their southern tour, having previously beaten Chatham. The weather was fine and there were approximately 8,000 spectators at the ground.

### Royal Arsenal v Nottingham Forest, 31 March 1891

Play in the first half was fast but even, and although the visitors fired numerous close shots, Bee on each occasion saved brilliantly. There was no score at half-time.

It was apparent that the pace had taken its toll on the home team, as their efforts in the second half were rather ragged. Consequently

*willing to meet professional teams in the north? (cheers).
He thought the Royal Arsenal was to be congratulated on
their honesty in taking the course they had taken
(applause). They could if they would, have driven the
proverbial coach and four through the London Football
Association Rules. He knew that there were many clubs
paying very liberal travelling expenses. If the resolutions
were passed there would be a succession of clubs, who
would form a little family party of their own.*

*Mr N. C. Bailey (Old Westminsters) briefly supported
the motion.*

*Mr. W. Jackson (Chairman of the Royal Arsenal FC)
who attended as the representative of the White Hart,
said he opposed the resolution on behalf of workingmen
in the sense of those who blackened their hands for a
living. He thought that the workingmen of the Arsenal
were the best judges of this particular case. Speaking as a
late member of the council, he expressed the opinion that
if these motions had been considered by a full committee
they would not have been presented in the form in which
they saw them in that evening. There were ten members
present out of a Council of twenty-eight, and the majority of the ten were totally ignorant of the business when
they arrived in that room. It was the narrow amateur
laws of the London Association which had compelled
them to take the steps they had. He on behalf of his club,
which was only a very small one – (laughter) – asked the
meeting to reject this motion. Let any club abstain from
playing with professionals if they so desired, but let them
not pass resolutions which would lower them in the eyes
of the whole sporting world. These motions were of the
principle of boycotting, which was offensive to every
Englishman (cheers). Directly the Arsenal Club reached a
certain standard there was a demand for their players.
Last year he believed they lost one of their players
through the rapacity of a northern team, but they did not
then propose to take any steps in defence, they were
prepared to lose their best men one after another. That
was the time when the true amateurism of the gentlemen
who now supported this motion should have come
forward to defend those who had not the education or*

*ability to defend themselves in the way these gentlemen had (loud cheers).*

*Mr. J. Starr (East Laboratory Swifts) opposed the motion.*

*Mr N. L. Jackson in reply, was of the opinion that a good field was open to amateur teams who wished to tour in the south and west, and that the north might be left to the professional element. Mr. Jackson then proceeded to rebuke Mr. Alcock for not having attended the Council meeting, at which those present were unanimous in their opinions.*

*Mr. Alcock said that he had never been summoned to that special meeting; still he thought that he had a perfect right to express his opinions etc – (cheers) – and he added that he should resign the London Football Association.*

*Mr. Jackson proceeded to say that football stood by itself as regards professionalism and amateurism. Cricket was out of this question (oh).*

*The Chairman called upon the meeting to divide, when the resolution was lost by 76 voting against and 67 for.*

*The Council's second proposition which ran as follows, was abandoned:*

*That no Club belonging to this Association shall play against a Club or player who has, since the passing of this rule played with or against any professional club having its headquarters in the south of England.*

Many would say that the argument over professionalism stemmed from the north/south divide. Charles Clegg, an amateur player for Sheffield (later Sir Charles Clegg, President of the FA 1923–7) played for England against Scotland in the first ever International on 30 November 1872. He recalled that 'none of the southern amateurs spoke to me so I wouldn't play again'.

According to the *Kentish Mercury* of 12 June 1891:

> **Royal Arsenal Football Club – Adjourned General Meeting (Extract)**
> *The adjourned General Meeting of the Members of the Club was held at the Freemasons Hall, Mount Pleasant, Plumstead, on Saturday evening, to consider the proposed alterations and additions to the rules, election of officers,*

*etc. Great interest was again evinced in the proceedings, there being some three hundred members present. Mr. A. Singleton occupied the Chair, and amongst those present were Messrs. G. Osborne, J. Humble, A. Brown, W. B. Jackson, W. Thompson, W. Dobbins, F. W. Beardsley, J.W. Julian, P. Connolly, H. Barbour etc.*

### Election of Officers
*The election of officers next took place and resulted as follows; those marked with an asterisk being elected:-*
*Chairman – \*W. B Jackson 207 votes; W. Davis 17.*
*Vice-Chairman – \*F.W. Beardsley 163 votes; J. Humble 65.*
*Committee – \*A. Singleton 160 votes; \*H. Steward 150; \*W. Thompson 141 votes; \* G. Lawrence 125 votes; \*W. Parr 118 votes; \*J. Hill 104 votes; \*J. Humble 102 votes; \*G. Smith 102 votes; W. Reid 101 votes; F.B. Hills 89 votes; H. Smith 81 votes; H. B. Weeks 83 votes; W.H. Lucas 63 votes; W.J. Dunn 57 votes; J.B. Reavill 38; W. Davis 23 votes; J. Plume 19 votes; W. Webb 19 votes; C. Shipman 17 votes.*
*The following were elected without opposition:-*
*Secretary Mr. G. H. Osborne; Assistant Secretary Mr. A. Brown; Financial Secretary Mr W. Dobbins.*
*Mr. Osborne thanked the Members for their renewal of confidence in him. In acknowledging the monetary award that had been made to him, he said he had always been glad to do all he could for the club, and that gratuitously, but was extremely grateful for what they had voted him. Messrs. W.B. Jackson, A. Brown, W. Dobbins and F. Beardsley also returned thanks.*

### The London Association and the Arsenal Club
*Mr W.B. Jackson the Club's delegate to the London Football Association gave an account of the meeting of that body at which he was present. He stated that the resignation of the Arsenal was accepted, and a long discussion took place as to whether his membership as the representative of the Arsenal Club should cease and by a majority of one it was decided it should whereupon he claimed to remain as a member of another club, and the discussion on that point was adjourned.*

*In conclusion Mr. Jackson paid a high compliment to the press generally for the stand they had taken with the Arsenal Club.*

*Other matters of detail having been discussed, a vote of thanks to the Chairman brought the proceedings to a close at a late hour.*

The penalty kick was officially introduced in 1891 following a blatant handball on the goal line by a Notts County Player in the FA quarter final against Stoke. Penalties did not find favour with all, many amateur players opting to kick the ball wide of the goal. The original idea for the penalty kick was believed to have been the idea of goalkeeper William McCrumm of Milford FC, County Armagh. The first penalty kick was thought to have been taken at Milford in 1890.

# Chapter 6

From the *Kentish Mercury*, 31 July 1891:

*Woolwich Arsenal Football Club – The Prospect of the Ensuing Season*

*Although a month will elapse before the now famous 'Reds' make their reappearance on the football field, we think it would not be out of place to give a short account of the teams to be encountered in the forthcoming season. The list of fixtures is a very formidable one, only six of the southern teams – Casuals, Crusaders, Clapton, London Caledonians, Chiswick Park and St. Bartholomew's Hospital – which figured in last season's programme being included in this year's, each of which the Arsenal defeated.*

*Cambridge University, whom the 'Reds' decisively defeated last December, will appear at Plumstead twice, whilst the Arsenal's old rivals – Chatham – are once more to be encountered. The Old Carthusians, at whose hands the 'Reds' sustained their reverse in the semi-final of the London Charity Cup competition after two drawn games, appear for the first time in the club's fixtures; and the representative team to be sent from Canada will be met at Plumstead. Of the other clubs with which the 'Reds' did battle last season, matches have been arranged with Sheffield United, Gainsborough Trinity, Sunderland, and Everton; with first named of these the Arsenal played a drawn game of one goal each, they defeated Gainsborough Trinity by two goals to one, and sustained reverses at the hands of the latter two. The fresh fixtures include matches with Preston North End, West Bromwich Albion, Birmingham St. George, Bootle, Grimsby Town, Stoke, Wolverhampton Wanderers, Burton Swifts, Crewe Alexander, Glasgow Rangers and other leading provincial Scottish clubs.*

*The team, as our readers are aware from the detailed reports which have appeared in our columns from time to time, will be a professional one, with an entirely new set of forwards. Of last year's team, those who have already signed on are the following:-*

*E. Bee, goal; J. McBean, back; and W. Stewart, D. McHardy, D. Howat and J.W. Julian halfbacks; and to this list we expect shortly to add the names of P. Connolly the well known back. The new forwards contain some first class men, in fact all may be classed under this heading: - B.L. Shaw (late of Sheffield United who gave a fine exhibition of the game when playing against Arsenal last year), A. Pearson (Ardwick and Dundee Our Boys), James Paton (Aston Villa and Vale of Leven), T. Graham (Vale of Leven) and the brothers J. and W. Welsh (Pollockshaws), 'Sandy' Robertson the former Preston North End player would occasionally assist, the first two will arrive at Plumstead early in August, and the others about the 16th of the same month. From the rapid stride the Arsenal have made in the football world and strengthened by a capable forward division, the 'Reds' with their old back division may, under the new arrangements, be expected to hold their own fairly well against their powerful opponents. The performance of the Club will be watched with the greatest interest and will no doubt attract even larger crowds to the Invicta grounds than was the case last season. Practice will probably commence at the Manor Field on Thursday 6th August.*

The Welsh brothers failed to make an appearance and subsequently refunded their signing on bonus of £40. New professional players for the 1891/2 season were:

**Andrew Rankin,** fullback; born 1870 in Hamilton. Height 5 ft 9 in, weight 11 stone 12 lb. A nibbler by trade (colliery wagon shunter). Previous clubs: Merryhill, Cowlairs, Airdrieonians and Northern of Glasgow.

**Frederick Collins,** fullback; born 1867 in Birmingham. Height 5 ft 5 in, weight 10 stone 2 lb. Toolmaker. Previous clubs: Wolverhampton Town and Wolverhampton Druids.

**David Durward McHardy,** centre halfback; born 1870 in Monifieth, Forfar. Height 5 ft 4½ in, weight 10 stone 11 lb. Ironmoulder. Previous club: Dundee East End.

**James Paton,** centre forward; born 27 March 1867 in Bonhill. Height 5 ft 8 in, weight 11 ½ stone. Flat press printer. Previous clubs: Vale Wanderers, Vale of Leven and Aston Villa.

**Bernard Shaw**, outside right; born 1866 in Sheffield. Height 5 ft 10½ in, weight 11 stone 6 lb. Former Captain of Sheffield Wednesday, previous clubs: Wolverhampton Wanderers and Sheffield United.

**Gavin Crawford**, inside or outside right; born 1869 in Galston, Ayr. Height 5 ft 9 in, weight 11 stone. A driller by trade. Previous clubs: Fairfield Rangers and Sheffield United.

**David Edward McLaren**, inside right; born 1867 in Lochee, Forfar. Height 5 ft 6 in, weight 11 stone. A slater by trade. Previous clubs: Lochee, East End Dundee and Middlesbrough Ironopolis.

**Andrew Pearson**, inside left; born 1867 in Carmyllie. Height 5 ft 6 in, weight 11 stone 4 lb. A mill worker. Previous clubs: Our Boys and Ardwick.

**Thomas Graham**, left forward; born 1868 in Balloch, Dunbarton. Height 5 ft 10 in, weight 12 stone. Printfield worker. Previous clubs: James Town and Vale of Leven.

Later arrivals were:

**Robert 'Bobby' Buist**, fullback/centre half; born 5 October 1869 in Goven. A driller by trade. Previous clubs: Fairfield Rangers, Cowlairs and Clyde.

**George Alexander Davie**, centre forward; born 19 April 1864 in Cardross. Silkscreen printer. Previous clubs: Everton, Sunderland and Renton.

From the *Kentish Mercury*, 4 September 1891:

> *Tomorrow the Woolwich Arsenal Football Club enter on their new enterprise, viz. that of running a strictly professional team, when they open their 1891/92 season with the match versus Sheffield United at the Invicta Recreation Grounds, which should prove a very interesting contest, as last year the meeting of these teams ended in a drawn game of one goal each. The ground is now completed, and is greatly improved. The raised ground outside the rails at the entrance end will give the spectators a much better view of the game than that hitherto obtained from that end, and will also afford additional accommodation. The teams to be encountered are a formidable lot, as our readers will have seen from the list of fixtures already published; but opinion runs high that the now famous 'Reds' will render a good account of themselves. The whole of the forwards are a new set, and*

*having had some capital training and practice, will enter the field perfectly 'fit,' whilst the backs, always a capable body with several first class additions, will no doubt be able to hold their own. Should only fine weather favour the opening game a very large crowd may be expected. A band will be in attendance from 2 pm, and will play selections before and after the match as well as in the interval. Kick off at 3.30 pm.*

Sheffield United played in their normal red and white striped shirts.

**Woolwich Arsenal v Sheffield United, 5 September 1891**

For the first quarter of an hour the play was even. Then for a period Arsenal were contained in their own half, the defence played well, and the visitors should have scored several times. Shortly before half-time, after a brilliant run by Thomas on the right, Watson scored a goal for the Sheffielders. For about 15 minutes after half-time the home team played much better, and once or twice looked like scoring. Their play then became scrappy, and about 13 minutes before time, from a free kick in front of goal, Drummond scored a second goal. No further goals scored, the visitors won 2–0.

*Teams:*

**Woolwich Arsenal:** Bee, goal; McBean and Connolly, backs; Julian, McHardy and Howat, halfbacks; Graham and Pearson, left wing, Paton, centre, McLaren and Crawford, right wing forwards.

**Sheffield United:** Mowlett, goal; Cane and Lilley backs; Nesbitt, Hendry and Whitham, halfbacks; Thomas and Dobson, right wing, Needham, centre, Watson and Drummond, left wing, forwards.

Referee: A G O Kennedy (Kent County Association), Touch judges A Singleton and Hammond.

One of United's future goalkeepers was Billy 'Fatty' Foulke. He stood 6 ft 2 in and on joining Sheffield weighed almost 19 stone, which later increased to nearly 25 stone. He took size 12 boots and his shirt collar size was 24 inches, yet despite his weight, in 1897 he was selected to play for England. He was once reputed to have swung on the cross-bar, which then broke under his weight. He had a volatile nature and allegedly grabbed hold of an opposition centre forward and stood him on his head. On occasions he had been known to walk off the pitch if he felt that his defence was not making enough effort. The crowds idolized Billy but his colleagues could be fearful of him when he was in a bad mood. While he played for United he collected a League Championship medal and two Cup Winners' medals. After 11 years at Sheffield United he was transferred to Chelsea FC. One of the stories told of him at Chelsea was that the team had been invited to a meal; Billy unfortunately arrived first and by the time the rest of his teammates had arrived, he had eaten the dinners intended for all his colleagues.

In their first season as professionals Arsenal were banned from all competitions except the FA Cup. Sadly, in friendly games they often failed to obtain the necessary attendances to ensure financial security. While they were capable of thrashing the local sides, they mostly failed to win against stronger opposition. They were beaten by Gainsborough Trinity 4–1, St George's, Birmingham 5–1, Sheffield Wednesday 8–1, Preston North End 3–0 and Sheffield United 4–1.

Turning professional had unsettled those players who had joined Arsenal as amateurs and had been found work at the Arsenal factory. They were expecting to be paid as professional footballers, but were advised by the management that no additional wages would be available, and indeed were fortunate to have jobs. Albert Christmas, having sustained serious injury to both legs and being unhappy about the wages situation, took his leave of the Arsenal team while remaining a factory employee. Bill Julian was informed that new professional Sandy Robertson would be replacing him as captain, but the committee wished him to remain in the team. Bill, a man of principle, declined and said he would prefer to captain the reserves.

In 1892 Arsenal formed a limited company with a nominal capital of 4,000 £1 shares and were elected to the Football League. The Corinthian Challenge took place; goal nets were used in the FA Cup Final for the first time; Division Two of the Football League was formed; and penalty takers were not allowed to play the ball twice.

The most important event that year for David and Georgie Danskin was the birth of their son William Leonard Danskin, called Billy, and born on 1 April 1892. Thankfully he appeared to be a healthy, lively boy.

The premier amateur club, the Corinthians, issued their famous 'Challenge', and offered to meet any other club at football, cricket and athletics, the proceeds to go to charity. The Barbarian Rugby Football Club accepted and beat the Corinthians at cricket by four wickets. The Corinthians then reversed the situation by winning 6–1 at association football, and just managed to win the athletics by one point. They then surprised everyone by beating the rugby players at their own game by 14 points (2 goals and 2 tries) to 12 (2 goals and 1 try).

A large crowd assembled in the Coventry Road enclosure, Birmingham for the appearance of Arsenal FC on Saturday to play their tie in the English Cup competition. The day was raw and cold, and the ground was in a very unsafe condition because of frozen ice and snow, making it both dangerous and difficult for the men to play upon. Consequently the standard of play was below that which might be expected from the teams.

---

**Small Heath (later Birmingham City) v Woolwich Arsenal, 18 January 1892**

Small Heath were fortunate in winning the toss and were helped considerably during the first half by a very strong wind blowing into the Arsenal goal. Davie started the game for the Reds. Jenkins headed back and the Heathens' right wing intercepted the ball. Two attempts to score failed when the ball went behind.

Crawford took possession from the goal kick and finished a clever run with a good shot at goal; the ball skimmed the cross-bar and went over. The Heathens attacked and Bee defended his goal well. Peachey, by some clever dribbling, passed his opponent but fell within shooting distance. The home team forced a corner off Bee, and from a scrimmage the Heathens scored the first goal. This enabled Small Heath to become the aggressors and pile on the pressure for some minutes, but the Reds' defence was brilliant, with Bee saving three shots in marvellous fashion; one of these, a long shot by Jenkins, might have beaten any goalkeeper.

The wind now became very strong. Bee stopped another swift shot from Jenkins but failed to stop one from Hallam and a third from Sheldon. Graham and Peachey then put in a neat combined run. A foul was given against Small Heath, and the opportunity to score was lost. The Heathens kept up the attack on the Reds' goal but Bee, showing good form, saved in rare style. McBean and Connolly found difficulty in sending the ball any distance up the ground. Scrimmage after scrimmage followed, but Crawford at last cleared. Bailey put in a long kick and McBean, missing the return, let in Walton who scored a fourth goal with a stinging shot. Peachey and Davie, despite the wind, put in some clever play and made a fierce raid on the home goal, but Charlesley cleared well. Peachey again made a good run but was held off by Speller. Hallam put in a long shot that just missed the goal. The score at half-time was Small Heath 4, Arsenal 0.

By the start of the second half the wind had dropped considerably, which was of no benefit to the Arsenal. Robertson changed the attack, switching Connolly and Peachey. This did not appear to be for the better as Hallam scored almost immediately. The Reds were given a corner but Connolly shot behind. Crawford forced another corner but Shaw also sent the ball behind. A free kick to the Reds, placed well by Howat, came close to the home goal but Jenkins got the ball away. The Reds were determined to score, and after Charlesley had saved a long shot by Crawford, Davie scored. Arsenal attacked again with good play by Shaw and Crawford, who shot the ball high over the cross-bar. Hallam staved off another attack by the visitors, and after running through, crossed to Morris who nearly scored, Bee putting the ball against the bar. A foul was given against Small Heath but Shaw failed to score. From the goal kick, the Heathens went away and after a scrimmage in front of the Arsenal goal Morris pushed the ball through and scored their fifth goal. Fifteen minutes before the end of the game, Shaw left the field injured. Small Heath beat Arsenal 5–1.
*Teams:*
**Small Heath:** Charlesley, goal; Bailey and F Spellar, backs; Ollis, Jenkins and Devey, halfbacks; Hallam and Walton, right wing, Morris, centre, Weldon and Hands, left wing forwards.
**Woolwich Arsenal:** Bee, goal; Connolly and McBean, backs; Robertson (captain), Buist and Howat, halfbacks; Shaw and Crawford, right wing, Davie, centre, Graham and *C H Peachey, left wing forwards.
* amateur player

The formation of the Arsenal team continued to change and for a friendly game against Windsor Phoenix in January, Goodun and Gardener were taken from the Reserves.

**Woolwich Arsenal v Windsor Phoenix, 21 January 1892**
The holders of the Bucks and Berks Cup yesterday appeared for the first time at the Invicta Recreation Grounds, Plumstead, to oppose a team of the Arsenal Club. Rankin made his reappearance for the home team. In the first half Pearson soon scored for the Reds but shortly after Benstead equalized for the visitors. McLaren then added a second for the Reds, who at half-time were leading 2–1. The second half was even more stubbornly contested, and it was just before the whistle sounded for time that Crawford scored the third goal for the Reds, which left them victorious 3–1.

*Team:*
**Woolwich Arsenal:** Goodun, goal; Gardener and Rankin, backs; Robertson (captain), Buist and Collins, halfbacks; Crawford and Pearson, right wing, Davie, centre, Graham and McLaren, left wing forwards.

The appearance of Grimsby Town at the Invicta Recreation Grounds, Plumstead, on Saturday 23 January attracted some 4,000 spectators. In the 1888–9 FA Cup, Grimsby had reached the second round proper. They had that season decisively beaten Burton Swifts, and the latter in turn had defeated Small Heath, so that from the result of the Arsenal Cup-tie it looked as though the Reds' chances of success in the contest were very remote.

**Woolwich Arsenal v Grimsby Town, 23 January 1892**
The Reds, however, appeared a very different team from that which was defeated at Birmingham. They played brilliantly together throughout, had considerably the best of the game, and won 4–1. The whole of the Arsenal team played a good game. Rankin (who had reappeared in the team on the previous Thursday) played very well, his tackling and kicking being first class. Buist and Howat were in fine form, each playing with great pace, some of the former's play being simply marvellous, while it is doubtful whether Howat ever played a better game than he did that Saturday. Of the forwards, Connolly, who played outside right, was the most prominent during the first half, putting in numerous brilliant single-handed runs and fine centres, but in the second half he seemed to fade. Davie played a great game throughout, while Crawford, Graham and Pearson frequently played well. Of the visiting team Murrell, Reddoch, and Ackroyd were by far the best. Arsenal's goals were scored by Davie (2), Connolly (1), and Crawford (1).
*Teams:*
**Woolwich Arsenal:** Bee, goal; Rankin and McBean, backs; Robertson, Buist and Howat, halfbacks; Crawford and Connolly, right wing, Davie, centre, Graham and Pearson, left wing forwards.
**Grimsby Town:** Ogilvie, goal; Lundie and T Frith, backs; Murrell, Walker and Reid, halfbacks; Smalley and C Frith, right wing, Reddoch, centre, Ackroyd and Haines, left wing forwards.
Referee: F J Wall.

Later that year, Grimsby Town became one of the founder members of the Football League Second Division together with Small Heath,

Sheffield United, Darwen, Ardwick, Burton Swifts, Northwich Victoria, Bootle, Lincoln City, Crewe Alexandra, Burslem Port Vale and Walsall Town Swifts. Not surprisingly, the first year's champions were Small Heath.

In February 1892 a meeting in London was called by Arsenal FC regarding forming a southern league, initially with 12 teams, including Arsenal, Reading, Millwall and Swindon. All the prospective members' representatives agreed to the new competition, but later after pressure from the London FA, the clubs withdrew their applications.

On 12 March 1892 the FA Cup Final took place at the Kennington Oval between West Bromwich Albion and Aston Villa. In the previous Cup final between these teams held in 1887, the local *Birmingham Press* commented on the excess gambling on the match, stating 'that many working men staked whole weeks' wages on the game'. The gate for that match had been 16,000. Allegedly in the 1892 final, where the gate was 25,000, even more money was wagered.

The firm favourites for this final were Aston Villa, who had beaten the League Champions, Sunderland, 4–1 in the semi-final. In the other semi-final, West Bromwich Albion were forced to replay non-league Nottingham Forest twice before qualifying for the final. (In the Football League that season, Aston Villa finished fourth from top while West Bromwich Albion finished third from bottom.)

Aston Villa were outplayed in nearly every position, with their goalkeeper, Warner, conceding three soft goals in the first half of the match. The final score was West Bromwich Albion 3, Aston Villa 0. Many allegations were made regarding match fixing and Warner, who was a publican, had the windows of his pub smashed. The Aston Villa players strongly denied any wrongdoing.

That summer Bill Julian decided to move to Luton Town FC as captain and coach. Luton was also a new professional side. Their Secretary/Manager was Julian's old friend and colleague at Boston Town, 'Pickles' Smith.

A few of David Danskin's old friends and associates suggested that he should stand for election to the Club Committee, and against his better judgement he agreed.

Extract from the *Kentish Mercury*, 17 June 1892:

### Woolwich Arsenal Football Club – Annual General Meeting
### Secretary's Report
*The following players had been engaged for next season –*
*Bee, goal; Rankin, Jeffrey and Earle, backs; Howat and*

Buist halfbacks, Henderson, Crawford, Davie, Booth and Elliott, forwards. The new players were: Earle who was a left back at Millwall Athletic, Henderson came from the Glasgow Rangers, and was reported to be one of the best outside rights in Scotland. Booth was late of Wolverhampton Wanderers, and Elliott was from Accrington. Jeffrey was a former teammate of Julian's at Boston. They were in communication with two other forwards and another halfback. Mr G. J. Groves the halfback had promised to assist the club when they desired his services (cheers). The next season's fixtures were discussed.

Mr Osborne reported that the Committee had, that afternoon, met Mr Weaver who said that at the end of next season, he would be prepared to let the ground for the whole of the next season provided the Arsenal formed a good Athletic Club, as he was anxious to see the club that held the ground the best in the metropolis (applause). He also said that if they took the ground for the season, and found at the end of the season that they could not conveniently pay the rent, he would be willing to let the balance go forward to the next season (cheers).

After a few remarks from several members the report was adopted unanimously.

### Secretary's Resignation

Mr G. H. Osborne, in resigning the Secretaryship, said that as the Club went on he found its work had increased and as his time was so much taken up with work in the Arsenal he was obliged to resign his position. He thanked the Committee and Members for their support during his period of office.

Election of Officers – Voting resulted as follows:-
Chairman – W.B. Jackson 281, F.W. Beardsley 66, W. Davis 62.
Secretary – H. Smith 253, H. Greenwood 147.
Assistant Secretary – A. Brown (without opposition).
Financial Secretary – W. Dobbins (without opposition).
Committee (5) – W. Lawrance 352, H. Greenwood 250, F.W. Beardsley 221, A. McQueen 156, J. W. Humble 145, H. Barbour 135, J. Hill 109, S. Ward 99, W. Davis 87, W. Reid 83, D. Danskin 78, W. Parr 77, A. Singleton 73, G.

*Smith 30, J. Maude 15, C. S. Heithersay 14.*
  *The meeting closed with votes of thanks to the old
Committee, Auditors and Chairman.*

What was noticeable was the lack of support for Alf Singleton, who
the previous year polled the highest committee vote.

Further additions to the team were two Scots: Frank Dyer, a halfback from West Bromwich Albion, and Duncan Gemmell, a forward
from Sheffield Wednesday.

In October Arsenal beat the Highland Light Infantry 3–0 in the first
qualifying round of the FA Cup competition. In the next round they
were to play City Ramblers. Although Arsenal was expected to win,
approximately 6,500 spectators were to witness the match. The
weather was reasonable.

> **Woolwich Arsenal v City Ramblers, 29 October 1892**
> Play had only been in progress 17 minutes when Elliott scored the
> first goal for the Reds. Three minutes later Davie scored a second.
> Shortly afterwards a third was added by Elliott. Henderson scored
> two more and at half-time the 'Reds' led by 5–0. Five minutes from
> the restart Booth had two more, then Nolloth scored the Ramblers'
> only goal. This was followed by three more goals scored by Hender-
> son, Booth and Elliott, the final result being 10–1 to the Arsenal.
> *Teams:*
> **Woolwich Arsenal:** Wood, goal; McQuilkie and Jeffrey, backs;
> Howat, Buist and Dyer, halfbacks; Crawford and Henderson, Davie,
> Elliott and Booth, forwards.
> **City Ramblers:** Morton, goal; McGabey and Goodwin, backs;
> Mordin, Butler and Brady, halfbacks; Buckley, Meggs and Nolloth,
> Withington and Peace, forwards.
> Referee: W H Harding.

On 8 November 1892 the Arsenal goalkeeper Edmund Bee married
Elizabeth Walford at the Woolwich District Registry Office. Elizabeth
was a local girl, the daughter of William Walford, a Plumstead
butcher.

For several weeks the main topic of conversation in the local pubs
had been the forthcoming FA Cup third round qualifying match
between Woolwich Arsenal and Millwall Athletic. Competition
between these two powerful local sides had always been maintained.

Millwall arrived with an army of dockers all wearing blue

rosettes, which contrasted well with the red of the ammunition workers. Although a large crowd had been expected, no one could have forecast that the attendance would be as high as 13,500, plus a large number viewing for free on the high bank overlooking the ground.

Five days earlier Arsenal had been beaten at home 4–0 by the League Champions Sunderland in a friendly, and although outclassed, the Reds had performed well. The same team was selected to play Millwall. The Athletic had strengthened their side by the inclusion of Hyslop of the Second Scots Guards and the London Caledonian captain, William Hay, a hard kicking and tackling fullback. He was an unusually large man for a Glaswegian, with a height of 6 ft 1½ in and weight of 13 ½ stone.

The weather was good for the time of year. Millwall played in blue and white striped shirts.

### Woolwich Arsenal v Millwall Athletic, 19 November 1892

Both teams were loudly cheered when they arrived on the pitch. Caygill, the Millwall goalkeeper and captain, won the toss and Davie started the game for the Reds against the wind and sun. Millwall began in a resolute manner, and within ten minutes Hyslop had passed to Jones, who then beat Bee, to the large cheers of the Millwall supporters. Arsenal counter-attacked strongly, and Henderson made several hard shots at goal, all of which were saved by Caygill. Fifteen minutes before half-time, the Arsenal managed to score in an unusual way. Caygill caught the ball from a shot by Booth but before he could clear, the five Arsenal forwards rushed in and attempted to force him and the ball into the goal. This was made more difficult because Caygill dropped to his knees and hugged the ball. The incident very much resembled a rugby scrum as the goalkeeper was rolled over into the goal, making the score 1–1. This success encouraged the Reds to play with greater determination, and when Hay cleared a shot from Davie, Howat took possession of the ball and scored the second goal for Arsenal, making the half-time score 2–1.

A few minutes after the restart the home side took the initiative, but again Caygill defended and cleared well. Rankin missed his kick and let in Hyslop, who gave Bee a stinging shot to clear, which he did with some difficulty. Millwall then pressed for a few minutes, and Green passed to Jones, who scored their second goal. Shortly after, Hyslop again put the ball into the net but the goal was disallowed for offside. For the next 15 minutes a bombardment was kept up on the visitors' goal during which Caygill defended extremely well, clearing shots from Elliott, Booth, Henderson and Gemmell in quick succession. At last Henderson managed to get the ball past Caygill, putting the Arsenal ahead. From then until the end of the match the Reds had the best of the play, and they won 3–2.

Undoubtedly Arsenal was the better side. Their short and neat passing contrasted totally with the long passing and untidy rushes of Millwall.

*Teams:*

**Woolwich Arsenal:** Bee, goal; Rankin and Jeffrey, backs; Howat, Buist and Dyer, halfbacks; Gemmell, Henderson, Davie, Elliott and Booth, forwards.

**Millwall Athletic:** Caygill, goal; Hay and Ingram, backs; Thompson, McMillan and Duke, halfbacks; McCulloch, Jones, Lindsay, Green and Hyslop, forwards.

Referee: R Evans, Hotspur.

Two years later Millwall were founder members of the Southern League, which for a time became almost as important as the Football League.

On Saturday 10 December Arsenal were down to play their old adversaries Clapton in the FA Cup. A former Arsenal player, Humphrey Barbour, was to play for Clapton. These clubs met on Saturday at the Invicta Recreation Grounds, Plumstead to play their tie in the final round of the qualifying competition of the FA Cup. Clapton had the choice but decided to play on their opponents' ground. The two defeats the Arsenal had inflicted on Clapton that season, however, did much to minimize the interest in the match, as only some 4,000 spectators were present. Ambler replaced Bee in goal for the Reds.

**Woolwich Arsenal v Clapton, 10 December 1892**

During the opening ten minutes of the game Clapton were twice dangerous without reaching Ambler. Then a long period of pressure by the Reds followed, but it was almost half-time before Henderson scored the first goal for the Reds, who having dominated could only lead 1–0 on changing ends. The second half continued similar to the first half: the Arsenal forwards applied enormous pressure but this in turn was contained by the Clapton defence. Booth added a second goal. Then the ball hit one of the Clapton backs for an own goal. In the end the Reds won 3–0.

*Teams:*
**Woolwich Arsenal:** Ambler, goal; Rankin and Jeffrey, backs; Howat, Buist and Dyer, halfbacks; Gemmell, Henderson, Crawford, Elliott and Booth, forwards.
**Clapton:** W Baker, goal; W H Russell and O O Hayward, backs; R H Clark, A E Casselton and S Smith, halfbacks; H O Worrall, J Ide, H Barbour, J F Mitchell and H Briggs, forwards.
Referee: Lieutenant Simpson, Royal Fusilliers.

Arsenal's next match on Monday 12 December was a friendly against Mr R G Armitage's Eleven. The goalkeepers were Edmund Bee for Arsenal and Charlie Williams, a local lad, for the opposition. Williams excelled himself in the match, keeping the score down to 3–1 for the Arsenal.

The visit of the formidable Nottingham Forest eleven to the Invicta Recreation grounds that Saturday created considerable interest in the neighbourhood, and as a consequence some 6,000 spectators were present. The visitors played their full strength, and included their new goalkeeper Daniel Allsopp, but the Arsenal made several alterations. A trial was given to Williams of Lewisham St. Mary's in place of Bee, and Devine took Dyer's place as left half back, the latter playing centre forward. Owing to the colours of the two teams being the same, the Arsenal players played in striped shirts.

**Woolwich Arsenal v Nottingham Forest, 17 December 1892**
Nottingham Forest attacked briskly from the start, and Horace Pike scored after three minutes' play. Two minutes later McInnes scored a second goal, the ball passing through off Jeffrey. For the next 25 minutes the home team played fairly well, but could not prevent Oscroft scoring for a third time.

The second half of the game saw the Arsenal improve their play, Booth, Elliott and the backs doing good work. A free kick for 'hands' to the Arsenal some 25 yards from the visitors' goal was taken by Buist, and from a good centre Dyer put the ball through and scored the first goal for his side. The Arsenal kept up the pressure, and it was not long before 'hands' were given against Forest almost in the mouth of the goal. This decision was strongly disputed by the visitors, but Henderson smartly added a second goal for the home side. The visitors then attacked, but some fine goalkeeping by Williams prevented them from scoring. Towards the close a corner fell to the Arsenal, and

Booth made a grand attempt to equalize but just failed. In the end Nottingham Forest won 3–2. Taken altogether the Arsenal eleven gave an encouraging display, combining well together from start to finish. A word of praise must be accorded to Williams for his goalkeeping: considering this was his first appearance in the company of first-class players his display promised well for the future.

*Teams:*

**Woolwich Arsenal:** Williams, goal; Rankin and Jeffrey, backs; Howat, Buist and Devine, halfbacks; Gemmell, Henderson, Dyer, Elliott and Booth, forwards.

**Nottingham Forest:** Allsopp, goal; Earp and Ritchie, backs; McCracken, McPherson and Smith, halfbacks; Higgins, W Smith, Oscroft, Pike and McInnes, forwards.

Referee: Lieutenant Simpson. Linesmen: Scott (Nottingham Forest) and Crawford (Arsenal).

On the same day, the Reserves were playing away at Chatham against the Chatham League. The team was Bee in goal, McQuilkie and Earle, backs; Watts, McKenzie and Stewart, halfbacks; Connolly, Sankey, Paton, Kirk and Stacey (forwards). Arsenal lost 2–1.

Edmund Bee left that summer to join his old friend Bill Julian at Luton FC in the Southern League. Besides playing, he assisted Julian with his soccer coaching. They were both to represent Luton in their successful 1893–4 FA Cup run, reaching the first round proper.

Close upon 4,000 spectators were present at the Invicta Recreation Grounds on Saturday 7 January to witness the match between the Northern League Champions, Middlesbrough Ironopolis and the Arsenal. Previous to this game the visitors had won 17 consecutive matches, and it was consequently expected that they would easily beat the home team. Neither side was fully represented, Howat and Booth being unavailable and A McCreddie and Hughes absent from the visiting team.

### Woolwich Arsenal v Middlesbrough Ironopolis, 7 January 1893

The Reds won the toss, and decided, unusually, to play against the wind. In the first half play was fairly even, with the Reds' backs and the Middlesbrough goalkeeper Watts dominant. Devine restarted and the ball was rushed into the visitors' half, and a long kick by Jeffrey sent the ball a little wide of the posts. Play was then fast and even, but after some neat passing by Gemmell and Henderson, the ball was passed to Devine, who shot over the cross-bar. 'Hands' was given against the visitors and Elliott put in a sharp shot, but failed to score. Each goal was then in turn attacked and at length McArthur with a swift, low shot beat Williams and scored the first goal for Middlesbrough. This reverse caused the Reds to play with greater determination, and they pressed their opponents for some considerable time. Just before full time, McArthur scored a second goal with a long low shot, and Middlesbrough Ironopolis won 2–0.

*Teams:*

**Woolwich Arsenal:** Williams, goal; Powell and Jeffrey, backs; Rankin, Buist and Dyer, halfbacks; Gemmell, Henderson, Devine, Elliott and Hyslop, forwards.

**Middlesbrough:** Watts, goal, Elliot and Langley, backs; Chatt, McNair and Oliver, halfbacks; McArther, W McCreddie, Seymour, Cooper and Hill, forwards.

Referee: W B Jackson, Arsenal.

Middlesbrough Ironopolis's existence was very brief: they were founded in 1889 and in 1892 decided to combine with the older Middlesbrough club that had been founded in 1876. In 1892 the two integrated teams unsuccessfully applied for election to the Football League. The teams again separated. In the 1893–4 season Middlesbrough Ironopolis successfully applied to join the Second Division of the Football League. After one season they were forced to resign due to financial pressures and went out of existence.

In Arsenal's next match, the first round of the FA Cup, they had the awesome task of playing league champions Sunderland, who had been named 'the Team of all Talents' when they won 13 matches in a row during the 1891–2 season. Their team included the former England international Tom Porteous, and the cream of the Scottish players. Johnny Auld and R Smellie had been Scottish internationals when playing with Scottish clubs. J Doig, Jock Campbell and Captain Hugh Wilson were selected to play for Scotland some years later, as was the star of the team James Millar, a flying forward with a hard shot. (Prior to the advent of professionalism, Scots who played south of the border were automatically barred from the international team.) Irishman David Hannah at the age of 26 was in his prime, and although only 5 ft 6 in, was a fast winger or inside right. Four years later he successfully played for the Arsenal. He epitomized the Scots proverb 'that guid gear goes in small buik'. The Arsenal club travelled to Sunderland to play their tie on the Newcastle Road ground before some 5,000 spectators. Sunderland played in their normal red and white stripes.

**Sunderland v Woolwich Arsenal, 21 January 1893**
There was no doubt whatever of the result, and although the Reds were defeated 6–0 they gave the Wearsiders a much better game than was expected. Individually the Reds were good and were well trained, but they lacked the combination of their powerful opponents. The opening exchanges were by no means one-sided, but after only ten minutes, David Hannah scored Sunderland's first goal. Shortly afterwards a corner fell to Sunderland, and Campbell headed a good goal. Play was then even for a time. Booth put in several brilliant runs, and Buist was loudly applauded for some fine play, but although the ball was hovering round the home goal the Reds were unable to score. The Sunderland forwards then pushed the ball down to the other end and Campbell scored a third goal. Directly the ball was set in motion again Millar ran through and scored the fourth goal, and just before half-time he added the fifth.

In the second half the visitors began briskly. Despite being given plenty of openings by Buist and the halfbacks, the Arsenal forwards continued to squander their opportunities in front of goal. Sunderland returned to the attack, and during the last ten minutes several exciting scrummages took place in the Arsenal goalmouth. Powell, Jeffrey and Williams defended grandly, but from one attack, Millar ran through and scored the final goal. The match was not so one-sided as the 6–0 score indicated.

*Teams:*
**Sunderland:** Doig, goal; Porteous and Smellie, backs; Wilson, Auld and Gibson, halfbacks; Gillespie, Millar, Campbell, D Hannah and J Hannah, forwards.
**Woolwich Arsenal:** Williams goal; Powell and Jeffrey, backs; Rankin, Buist and Dyer, halfbacks; Howat, Henderson, Devine, Elliott and Booth, forwards.

On 25 January 1893 Arsenal played a friendly match against Oxford University. The university side were all amateurs, but nevertheless were a powerful team, and included Gilbert Smith (known as G O Smith), Charles Fry, W J Oakley and G B Raikes, all of whom were, or would be, England internationals. The Oxford defence and halfbacks were on average 13 stone and over 6 ft in height.

**Oxford University v Woolwich Arsenal, 25 January 1893**

The return match between these teams took place at Oxford on Wednesday; both teams were well represented. Oxford played in their usual dark blue and white halved shirts. In the first half the home team had the best of the game but they were not however able to score until just on half-time, when Smith obtained a goal from a penalty kick. During the second half the Reds played in a determined fashion, and time after time looked like scoring, but Raikes's defence was good, and no further points being obtained the university won 1–0.

*Teams:*

**Oxford University:** G B Raikes (Magdalen), goal, C B Fry (Wadham) and W J Oakley (Christchurch), backs; C B Alexander (Trinity), E C Bliss (Oriel) and T C Robinson (Oriel), halfbacks; C D Hewitt (Magdalen), R J Salt (New), G O Smith (Keble), J Walker (Magdalen) and F Street (Christchurch) (captain), forwards.

**Woolwich Arsenal:** Williams, goal; Powell and Jeffrey, backs; Rankin, Devine and Dyer, halfbacks; Howat and Henderson, Shaw, Elliott and Booth, forwards.

G O Smith played for England on numerous occasions and was known for his fantastic ball control and an instinct for locating team-mates with intelligent passing. He had a powerful shot using either foot. He later became one of the England team (all Corinthians) who beat Wales 5–1 in 1904. Smith was a sensitive person. When his close friend Oakley was knocked unconscious in an international match in Glasgow in 1900, he stayed behind until his friend was well enough to travel.

G B Raikes played four times for England in 1895–6, and is remembered for an unusual own goal when playing for Oxford University v Sheffield. His powerful goal kick hit one of his own defenders on the head and the ball rebounded into his goal.

This extract from the *Kentish Mercury*, 27 January 1893, describes the Half Yearly Meeting of the Woolwich Arsenal FC:

> *The Club and the Invicta Ground*
>
> *The members of the Woolwich Arsenal FC assembled in large numbers last evening at the Masonic Temple, Mount Pleasant, Woolwich, the occasion being the half-yearly meeting of the club. Mr W B Jackson (Chairman of the Club) presided, supported by Messrs Humble, Lawrence, Beardsley, McQueen, and Greenwood (Committee), H*

Smith (Secretary), A Brown (Assistant Secretary). The Chairman asked the meeting to pay the greatest attention to the questions that would be brought forward, and he asked their kind consideration in the conducting of the meeting. When the history of the club was written it would be said to have been one of the most important ever held in connection with the club. The Secretary read the Minutes that were adopted unanimously.

The Chairman said that he would give them the latest terms offered to the club by the proprietor of the ground. He had offered the club the ground for a fresh lease of £400 a year with rates and taxes of about £100 (cries of 'oh'). It would also be compulsory for them to take the ground for twelve months. After another interview with Mr Weaver's representative a little more favourable terms were offered – a rent of £350, all rates and taxes to be paid by the club, and the landlord to have a nominee on the committee ('oh oh'). The committee could not accept these terms, as the responsibility was too great, and they must ask their members to decide. He said again the question was the most serious that had ever presented itself to the club. The club was now paying a rental of £200 for eight months, the landlord paying rates and taxes.

Messrs King, Ward, Whiting and Baker having spoken, a resolution to the effect that Mr Weaver should be told that the club could not accept the terms offered, was proposed by Mr Whiting and seconded by Mr Hodgin.

Mr Humble said that since they had had the ground it has cost them £60 a year to keep the ground in good repair, whilst he had estimated that to have the ground put into proper repair and drained it would cost £250. They would thus have to pay £750 for the ground should they accept the terms offered.

Mr Singleton said they had seen the black side of the question and he would now look at the other side. They could let the ground out for various purposes in the summer, then they could form an athletic club of their own, and make something out of athletics.

Mr McQueen said that if the committee advised them to accept Mr Weaver's terms, they would be traitors to the club. The present rent was as much as they could afford.

The Chairman reported that they had been informed that Sunderland paid £45 a year for their ground, the Wolverhampton Wanderers £76 a year, whilst the average of the professional clubs paid £100. He concluded by putting Mr Whiting's motion that was carried unanimously.

A motion moved by Mr Ward, that the meeting should appoint a Sub-Committee of five members to work in conjunction with the Committee to consider the question and report back in two weeks was also carried unanimously. A Sub-Committee was duly elected.

The meeting ended.

# Chapter 7

Arsenal's lease of the Invicta Recreation Grounds expired at the end of the 1892–3 season. Mr George Weaver, owner of the ground, was not prepared to accept Arsenal's offer of terms for renewal of the lease, so at a general meeting of the Arsenal FC it was agreed, after lengthy discussion, to purchase a new ground and transform the club into a limited liability company.

It was decided that the new ground should be in the vicinity of the old one, and at length the Manor Field, scene of the club's earlier triumphs, was purchased. At first it was thought that the ground could only be acquired on a yearly tenancy, but Mr J Morris of Hastings agreed to sell the freehold for £300 per acre. In all, about 13.5 acres were acquired for around the sum of £4,000.

Five and a half acres were enclosed as a football field. The land was not level by about 2 ft 4 in. Eight thousand loads of broken brick rubble were laid, and covered with 2½ in of loam. This was topped by well-drained turf to create a fine playing surface.

On the north side a wooden five-tiered terrace, 380 ft long, was erected with a 7 ft promenade in front. The Press Box, located in the centre of the terrace, gave a fine view of the whole ground, and could house about 12 reporters. The terrace could accommodate around 2,000 spectators.

The players' dressing rooms were located on the south side and built from galvanized iron, lined with matchboarding. The building was divided into three compartments: a room for the home team, one for the visiting team and a committee room. When not being used for football purposes, this would form a recreational area for players, where games, newspapers and periodicals would be provided.

Plans for a grandstand had been drawn up but this was not built at the same time because of difficulties in getting the plans passed by the London County Council. The proposed building was to be 80 yards by 20 ft and would be for the use of shareholders, with an extra charge being made for the general public. There would be three bars, one for non-intoxicating liquors. Three entrances would be in the Giffen Manorway, while two additional exits (one for shareholders), would be provided in the private road of the London County Council (subject to permission). The parish authorities would fill up the old ditch facing the main entrance, while steps were to be made down the embankment leading from the Plumstead Road to the lane. When all the works were complete, the ground would hold between 25,000 and 30,000 spectators.

James Cavey had organized a shuttle bus service from Woolwich Market to the Manor Grounds.

As far as finances were concerned, the company could hardly have been floated at a worse time owing to slackness of work in the Arsenal. However, the people of Woolwich and Plumstead readily supported the project, and out of the 3,000 £1 pound shares offered to the public, 2,600 were quickly taken up, being in the names of between 1,500 and 1,600 people. Another source of income additional to the gate, terrace and stand was from season tickets of around 1,400 at ten shillings and sixpence each.

The directors decided to base the team for the new season on the best players from the previous season, together with a few new players. The club re-signed Booth, Elliott, Shaw, Crawford, Gemmell, Henderson, Devine, Howat, Buist, Powell, Jeffrey and C Williams. The new men were Heath (late of Wolverhampton Wanderers and Wednesbury Athletic) and Davis (of Birmingham St George's) while Ambler, the ex-Clapton goalkeeper who had played in the reserves the previous season, had already signed the professional form.

The Club had also been admitted to the Second Division on their first application to join. The matter had been discussed in previous years, but the directors thought that doing so now, even accepting the extra travelling expenses that would be incurred, would be beneficial to the company. Not only would the games with the various league teams prove more attractive, but also no guarantee would be required. It was noted that the previous season the club had paid £1,345 as guarantees to visiting clubs, so shareholders could congratulate themselves on the wise step the directors had taken.

A very good list of fixtures had been arranged, in addition to matches with the clubs forming the Second Division of the League: Sunderland, Wolverhampton Wanderers, Burnley, Stoke, West Bromwich Albion, St Mirren, Chatham, London Caledonians, Casuals and Crusaders would be encountered, while several other clubs would be met whose names did not figure on the list. Arsenal was filled with confidence for the forthcoming season. The opening match took place at home on 2 September 1893 against Newcastle United, one of the most formidable teams in the Second Division.

Officials of the company were:

**Jack Humble**, Chairman. Besides being an active member of the football club, Jack was a member of the Vestry (local council), and also a member of the Radical Club which attempted to put pressure on local authorities for the good of the community in general. He later became a member of the Labour Party.

**Fred Beardsley**, Company Director. A former player, he also acted as chief scout, on occasion travelling as far as Scotland to watch prospective players.

**Arthur Brown**, Company Director. A former player who occasionally deputized for the secretary.

**Alfred McQueen**, Financial Director was an engineer.

**George Lawrence**, Financial Director, a newsagent (died 1900).

**Arthur Fowler**, Company Director (Ground). A surveyor by profession.

**James Henry Hodgin**, Company Director (Ground). A builder by trade.

**Henry Hodgin**, Company Director. Builder and father of James.

**Harry Greenwood**, Corresponding Secretary. An engineer.

**William Dobbins**, Secretary. An engineer.

**James Cavey**, Company Director (Ground). A former tenant of the Manor Field, James and his brother were the owners of many acres of land in the Plumstead/Woolwich area, including marshland. There were signposts erected to caution trespassers, but large gangs of men arriving in boats to shoot hares caused the brothers no end of trouble. The signs were totally ignored and were used for target practice. Occasionally a poacher was caught and prosecuted.

Notable shareholders were:

**Ellen Beardsley** ('Nellie'), wife of Fred, who strangely hated football, one share.

**Richard Bee**, engineer, who may have been of the original team, one share.

**Charles Duggan**, LCC employee, who may have been of the original team, one share.

**James G Hill**, tin-plate worker and early team member, one share.

**Arthur Humble**, pattern maker, brother of Jack, one share.

**Walter Lomax**, publican of the Dover Castle next door to the Fletchers, ten shares.

**William Parr**, turner and team manager, one share.

**Alexander 'Joseph' Smith**, turner and original team member, one share.

**James Moy,** blacksmith and original team member, one share.

**Edward Dinmore,** proprietor of the Coffee Tavern, and the biggest shareholder with 50 shares.

The new company was well supported by the English 'Royal Arsenal' veterans. Jack Humble, Arthur Brown and Fred Beardsley were appointed directors, and others became shareholders. The canny Scots were noticeable by their absence, and were later proved wise in not taking this business opportunity. The general feeling was that maybe the Club had progressed too fast. After all, it was only a few years earlier that they had been collecting money for their first ball. The men had immensely enjoyed their weekend escapades that took them away from the drudgery of the factory. Who cared if the attendance was poor that week? Of course once you were on the treadmill you needed more attractions just to maintain the interest of the supporters. David Danskin, for instance, was just as keen as ever about football, and enjoyed coaching and officiating in local matches.

When the Arsenal FC joined the Second Division of the Football League, the Woolwich Arsenal workers felt that there was a need for an amateur side to represent them against other local teams, so the Royal Ordnance Factories FC was formed. They played at the Invicta Grounds (what a come down for Weaver!). Five veteran Arsenal players joined the club: Connolly, McKenzie, McBean, George and Meggs. The first two named were unable to play until reinstated by the FA. Other players to join were Walker, the Marlow goalkeeper who was 6 ft 4½ in tall, Thomson, formerly with Millwall, Brian of Plumstead and Sawyer, late of Marlow. The club entered the Amateur Cup in its first year.

**Woolwich Arsenal v Newcastle United, 2 September 1893**

Joe Powell, the ex-army man captaining Arsenal for the first time, won the toss and chose to play with a slight breeze and the sun behind him. Thompson started the game for the visitors, and although the Arsenal forwards began well, Crate and Bowman soon took the ball to the other end for United, resulting in a corner. Williams fisted the ball away, and Jeffrey placed a long kick out to Booth who passed to Elliott, resulting in a poor corner. Crate and Bowman defended well and play was even. Six minutes into the game, Elliott and Booth set up a chance for Shaw who, with a good shot, cracked the ball into the net amidst tremendous cheering. A free kick to Arsenal was well placed by Powell but the ball was cleared. Newcastle, with a neat display of passing, put the ball into touch behind the Arsenal goal. Play was even for a while then Williams foiled Sorley's attempt to score. From a free kick, the Arsenal forwards attacked, with Henderson, Gemmell and Shaw playing well. Henderson was unlucky not to score. The Arsenal combined effectively and kept the ball in the United half until Wallace and Sorley cleared. Powell collected a loose ball and gave a long pass to the forwards. After a goal kick the visitors advanced and the ball was headed over the bar. Two well-taken corners were successfully deflected by Williams, and at half-time the score was 1–0 to Arsenal.

Shaw restarted. Gemmell put in a good shot that was pushed away by Ramsay. Play then went to the other end where Booth passed to Elliott, who put in a stinging shot and scored the second goal for the home side. Play was even for some time, then Wallace and Sorely combined well to take the ball towards the Arsenal goal, but Thompson moved into an offside position and the opportunity was wasted. United played in a determined manner but their efforts were strongly repulsed. Williams saved a corner, but a few minutes later was not so successful when a quick shot from Crate went into the net. The visitors continued to play well, and a free kick against the Arsenal in front of goal enabled Sorely to score. The game, well contested with both sides unsuccessfully trying for the winner, ended in a 2–2 draw.
*Teams:*
**Woolwich Arsenal:** Williams, goal; Powell and Jeffrey, backs; Devine, Buist and Howat, halfbacks; Gemmell, Henderson, Shaw, Elliott and Booth, forwards.
**Newcastle United:** Ramsay, goal; Jeffery and Miller, backs; Crielly, Graham and McKane, halfbacks; Bowman, Crate, Thompson, Sorley and Wallace, forwards.
Referee: J C Tillotson (Birmingham).

Liverpool made their first appearance at the Manor Grounds in October. They were the current unbeaten league leaders.

**Woolwich Arsenal v Liverpool, 28 October 1893**
The visitors won the toss and had the advantage of a strong wind. The first 30 minutes was fast and even. Liverpool was awarded a free kick, 50 yards from the home goal. McCartney placed the ball well, and it flew off Williams' leg into the net. The goal and problems with the wind seemed to demoralize the Reds. A long hard kick from the

middle of the pitch by M McQueen sailed, wind assisted, into the top of the home team's goal. This was followed shortly afterwards by another similar strike by H McQueen. Stott scored a fourth from a scrummage, and H McQueen, encouraged by his previous success, scored the fifth goal from another very long-range shot. At half-time the visitors led 5–0.

In the second half play became extremely rough. In one incident the referee cautioned Bradshaw for deliberately kicking Buist without attempting to play the ball. Naturally the home crowd thought Bradshaw should have been sent off. Play became very scrappy. Near the end of the match Williams made several good saves, which prevented Liverpool adding further to their score.

*Teams:*

**Woolwich Arsenal:** Williams, goal; Powell and Storrs, backs; Crawford, Buist and Howat, halfbacks; Shaw, Henderson, Heath, Elliott and Booth, forwards.

**Liverpool:** McQueen, goal; Hannah and McLean, backs; McCartney, M McQueen and McBride, halfbacks; Dick and McVean, Bradshaw, Stott and H McQueen, forwards.

Referee: Craven (Maidstone).

In the 1893–4 season an unbeaten Liverpool won promotion to the First Division of the Football League. The following season, 1894–5, they finished bottom of the First Division. They were a trifle unlucky as the bottom eight finished within a few points of each other.

In 1895–6 Liverpool were again promoted as champions from Division Two. This time they were better prepared and maintained their position in the First Division.

A few days after the defeat by Liverpool, Arsenal played the FA Cup holders, Wolverhampton Wanderers, in a friendly. The Arsenal had always enjoyed a good relationship with the Wolverhampton team, mainly due to the efforts of Jimmy Hill, which had generated a flow of players to Arsenal, including their latest capture Joe Cooper. The other new Arsenal players were amateurs. English-born C McGahey's previous club was City Ramblers, and he had also played cricket for Essex. He was 21, height was 6 ft 1 in and weight 14 stone 4 lb. Stanley Briggs, the other newcomer, had previously played for Tottenham. The Wanderers included their famous England international goalkeeper 'Billy' Rose. Wolves appeared to have sent a weakened side, with seven changes from the Cup-winning team. The attendance of 5,000 was good for a friendly.

**Woolwich Arsenal v Wolverhampton Wanderers, 30 October 1893**

The start was delayed approximately 20 minutes because of the late arrival of McGahey. The first half was slightly in favour of the Reds. Crawford was particularly prominent, unleashing some powerful shots that Rose had to be at his best to save.

In the second half, the Wolves played with ten men. Arsenal commenced in a determined manner, and from a long pass by Howat, Crawford raced through to score. For the remaining part of the second half, the extra man enabled the Arsenal to retain the edge. The crowd appreciated the sporting entertaining match, the final score being 1–0 to the Arsenal.

*Teams:*

**Woolwich Arsenal:** Williams, goal; McGahey and Storrs, backs; Devine, Briggs and Howat, halfbacks; Crawford and Henderson, Cooper, Elliott and Booth, forwards.

**Wolverhampton Wanderers:** Rose, goal; G Swift and Dunn, backs; Griffiths, Cheade and Davis, halfbacks; Woodhall and Grimm, Butcher, Wood and Black, forwards.

Referee: Baywell (Chatham).

That year Billy Rose was to found the Players Union. At the end of the 1893–4 season Billy and four other members of Wolves' Cup-winning side were rewarded with the sack. The Wolves directors later realized their mistake and persuaded 'Dickie' Baugh (former England international) and Billy to return. In the 1896 FA Cup Final they were both due to play, but Billy was injured. Sheffield Wednesday won the final 2–1.

In November Arsenal played Ardwick in a Second Division match. Williams had a foot injury, so Jeffrey, normally a fullback, took his place in goal.

**Woolwich Arsenal v Ardwick (Manchester City), 11 November 1893**

The standard of the game was poor. Ardwick began with a strong wind behind them. From a breakaway Storrs sent a powerful shot into the Ardwick goalmouth. Both Booth and Douglas went for the ball, the latter being winded. Henderson rushed in and scored. This was the only goal of the match, the result being 1–0 to the Arsenal.

*Teams:*

**Arsenal:** Jeffrey, goal; Powell and Storrs, backs; Devine, Davis and Howat, halfbacks; Crawford, Henderson, Cooper, Elliott and Booth, forwards.

**Ardwick:** Douglas, goal; Robson and McVicars, backs; Regan, Whittle and Middleton, halfbacks; Morris, Yates, Steel, Milarvie and Davies, forwards.

In the following season Ardwick shrewdly purchased goalkeeper Charlie Williams from Arsenal. Charlie was part of their Second Division Championship winning team in 1898–9.

Arsenal played Rotherham Town in Division Two, at home on 13 November 1893, and won the game 3–0. The Rotherham goalkeeper, Arthur Wharton, aged 28, was born in Ghana of mixed parentage. He was the first non-white player to appear for a Football League club. Arthur became a professional footballer in the 1890s after achieving fame as a sprinter, both amateur and professional. He won the Amateur Athletic Association 100 Yards Championship in 1886 and 1887, and in the former year equalled the then world record with a time of 10.0 seconds. From Rotherham he transferred to Sheffield United, but had little opportunity to make his mark as a goalkeeper in their League side because Billy Foulke was in such fine form. He returned to Rotherham after only one season. Sadly he died a penniless coal miner in 1930.

For the second year in succession Arsenal and Millwall were drawn together in the third qualifying round of the FA Cup. In the earlier rounds Arsenal had beaten Ashford University 12–0, then Clapton 6–2. Millwall had beaten Ilford 3–1 away in the previous round.

There was considerable local interest in the forthcoming match, and many saw the game as the championship of the south. The Arsenal Executive had made every effort to accommodate the anticipated large crowd. The gates were opened two hours before the advertised kick-off time. Special trains, trams, buses, steamboats, brakes and traps by the hundred had brought the 20,000 strong crowd to Plumstead. The previous season the teams had met three times, and on each occasion Arsenal had been successful with an aggregate score of 9–2.

**Woolwich Arsenal v Millwall Athletic, 25 November 1893**
Arsenal kicked off against the wind and as before, Millwall conducted the contest in their long kick and rush style and Arsenal using their

quick short passing game. At half-time Arsenal was leading by 1–0, the goal scored by Davis with a long high shot.

With the wind at their backs Arsenal dominated the second half. They failed to score through the defensive work of Obed Caygill, the Millwall captain and goalkeeper, ably assisted by Graham, one of his fullbacks. More sharpness in front of goal and Arsenal could have increased their score. The final score was Arsenal 1, Millwall 0.

*Teams:*

**Woolwich Arsenal:** Jeffrey, goal; Powell and Storrs, backs; Davis, Buist and Howat, halfbacks; Crawford, Henderson, Shaw, Elliott and Booth, forwards.

**Millwall:** Caygill, goal; Graham and Davies, backs; Aitken, Robertson and Willing, halfbacks; Wilson, Jones, Lindsay, Cunningham and Hollands, forwards.

Referee: Ashmole (Leicester Fosse). Linesmen: A Brown and W Kitson.

Obed Caygill (1870–1945) had previously been offered professional terms with Woolwich Arsenal but had wisely declined. He was later promoted from Senior Clerk to Docks Manager.

Obed Caygill

In the next qualifying round of the FA Cup Woolwich Arsenal played away, beating the Second Scots Guards by 2–1 after extra time. Arsenal was then drawn in the first round proper against Sheffield Wednesday. The Sheffield club was positioned in the lower half of the English First Division. Wednesday's star players were the veteran W Betts, a former England international, M J Earp of the famous Nottingham family and Fred Spikesley, who was to play seven times for England between 1893 and 1898.

**Woolwich Arsenal v Sheffield Wednesday, 27 January 1894**
Shaw kicked off for the Arsenal. The game commenced at a fast pace. Booth made a good run on the left but he hit the ball wide. After some scrappy play in front of the home goal, Spikesley scored an easy goal when Williams attempted to catch a high ball. Arsenal fought back and scored from another good run on the left by Elliott and Booth, ending in a well-struck high volley by Elliott, which beat Allan. The half-time score was 1–1.

For the first 30 minutes of the second half the Reds were forced to defend. A good run on the right by Webster and Davis provided the influential Spikesley with his second goal. Arsenal quickly responded and pushed hard for the equalizer, the Wednesday goal being bombarded. On one occasion a defender fisted out when the goalkeeper was beaten. The Reds' captain appealed for a penalty, but the referee strangely only awarded a free kick, much to the annoyance of the home players and crowd. The final result was 2–1 to Sheffield Wednesday. The referee was followed from the ground as he made his way to the railway station. The hostile crowd made their opinion known loudly.

*Teams:*

**Woolwich Arsenal:** Williams, goal; Powell and Jeffrey, backs; Davis, Buist and Howat, halfbacks; Crawford, Cooper, Shaw, Elliott and Booth, forwards.

**Sheffield Wednesday:** Allan, goal; Earp and Langley, backs; Brown, Betts and Jamieson, halfbacks; Webster, Davis, Woodhouse, Brady and Spikesley, forwards.

Referee: T Gunning (Hon Sec London Association).

Following the match, a protest was lodged by the Arsenal Executive at the decision of the referee in not awarding a penalty kick. This matter was discussed at a council meeting of the Football Association, Mr F Beardsley representing Woolwich Arsenal FC. Not surprisingly the referee's decision in giving a free kick was upheld. (Mr

Gunning was of course Honorary Secretary of the London FA, and no friend of Woolwich Arsenal.)

In the Cup Final that season, Notts County were the surprise winners, beating Bolton Wanderers 4–1. This was a record as County was then in the Second Division. Jimmy Logan scored a hat-trick. According to the *Nottingham Guardian*, County's training consisted of moderate exercise with dumb-bells and a bottle of stout each night! The final was played at Everton with an attendance of 32,000. Several teams that year entered both the FA Cup and the Amateur Cup, one of the notables being Tottenham Hotspur. From that season onwards the Old Boys' teams took no further interest in the FA Cup.

The league match against Newton Heath, which of course was William Campbell's old club, was said to be quite exciting. Two of the 'bad boys', Robbie Donaldson and George Perrins, were still playing for Newton Heath's first team. Former Airdrieonian Donaldson began his career with Newton Heath with a dispute, as Blackburn Rovers also claimed he had signed for them. Donaldson, who was a strong thickset man, had good ball control and was a prolific goalscorer with a high work rate. Newton Heath played in their red and white halved shirts. The attendance was approximately 5,000. This was the first match between these two sides.

### Newton Heath (Manchester United) v Woolwich Arsenal, 13 October 1894

Arsenal attacked strongly at the start. Perrins intercepted and cleared the ball into the visitors' half. Newton Heath was awarded a free kick, and Smith headed well into the Arsenal goalmouth but Storer saved. Immediately afterwards Donaldson put in a good shot, Storer again saving, at the expense of a corner. This proved abortive, and Arsenal cleared. Some neat passing ensued between the Arsenal forwards, but O'Brien shot rather clumsily. Shortly afterwards a miskick by McCartney let the Arsenal in, and although Douglas made a good attempt to save, Mortimer managed to net and scored Arsenal's first goal. For quite a period the visitors did most of the pressing, but Douglas ably repelled these smart attacks. Powell then cleared and the ball was collected by Boyd, who initiated a fine piece of passing by the Arsenal forwards. This ended when Donaldson tackled Buchanan. The ball was then driven towards the Arsenal goal, and Storer conceded a corner which was unproductive. This was followed by another period of clever passing by the Arsenal forwards, Mortimer adding the second goal for the visitors. At half-time the visitors led 2–0.

On resuming Newton Heath began well, Storer having to save twice in quick succession. Again the Heathens pressed, with Peters sending the ball into touch. Donaldson and Clarkin continued to attack but the Arsenal backs were equal to the task. Clarkin then headed the ball into the Arsenal goal, where it struck the underpart of the cross-bar and rebounded into play; the referee allowed the goal. Both teams then played with greater energy, and Storer gave a further example of his brilliant goalkeeping for which he was loudly applauded. Boyd and Mortimer then broke through the home defence and Mortimer beat Douglas with a good shot. Donaldson and Gow switched positions, which proved beneficial. Donaldson then scored the second and third goals. The final result was a 3–3 draw.

*Teams:*

**Woolwich Arsenal:** Storer, goal; Powell and Caldwell, backs; Stevenson, Boyle and Howat, halfbacks; Crawford, Buchanan, Boyd, O'Brien and Mortimer, forwards.

**Newton Heath:** Douglas, goal; McCartney and Erents, backs; Perrins, McNaught and Davidson, halfbacks; Clarkin, Donaldson, Dow, Smith and Peters, forwards.

Referee: Pennington (Burslem).

Following this match the *Manchester Evening News* reported that sadly, a section of the crowd standing behind the Bank Lane goal barracked the home goalkeeper and his backs. According to the press, this resulted in the defence not playing to their best ability at home. Newton Heath finished third that season, whilst Arsenal finished eighth.

Robbie Donaldson scored over 50 league goals while with Newton Heath from 1892 to 1897. He followed his friend George Perrins and joined Luton in 1897 for a reputed £80 transfer fee.

Several important engineering achievements were completed in 1894. Queen Victoria opened the Manchester Ship Canal, which had taken 25 years to build. Blackpool Tower and Tower Bridge became operational. The bridge, which was clad in granite and stone to match the nearby Tower of London, could open to allow large vessels into the Pool of London. Two 360 horse power steam engines housed in the two towers were the source of power, allowing the bridge to be opened and closed at regular intervals.

In December the Reverend Veazey in a sermon made a scathing attack on the Woolwich Local Board of Health, regarding lack of progress in improving housing conditions in the St Martin's District. 'At three houses in Artillery Place there were eighteen rooms, six of which were cellars occupied by ten families, in all 43 persons.' More examples were given. There was an instance where there was only one convenience for 24 persons. There was insufficient light and air. The Board was to later reply that they would investigate some of the complaints.

David Danskin and Georgie considered themselves fortunate: although they cooked on a solid fuel stove, they had the modern incandescent gas mantels for lighting. Their surviving son Billy was a healthy strong boy, thank goodness, and as could be expected, was spoilt by Georgie. He was an active child and as such his presence was not always encouraged at the Fletchers' busy bakery.

The Danskins' home in 1896

1895 was an eventful year in many ways. The River Thames froze, the FA Cup was stolen, and the Arsenal men were shocked and saddened by the death of an old friend and colleague. A now slower Jimmy Meggs had returned to play for City Ramblers. William Scott, the formerly brilliantly fast Royal Arsenal outside left, had been seriously ill for a considerable time, and Jack Humble organized a benefit concert at the Plumstead Radical Club and was allowed to use its hall free of charge. Both Fred Beardsley and David Danskin continued to referee local games. To qualify as a referee one needed to be sponsored by two FA approved clubs. In their case there was no problem because of their connections with both the Woolwich Arsenal and the Royal Ordnance.

The Arsenal continued to receive steady coverage of their games in the press, especially the *Kentish Mercury*. Of particular note is a report in January 1895, which stated the 'Woolwich Arsenal team *under the management of Mr W Parr*, would leave Euston at 6.30 pm and stay the night at Stoke, in preparation for the match at Burslem Port Vale'. It was anticipated that Arsenal would win the match, as only a few weeks earlier they had beaten the same team 7–0 at home. They duly won the away fixture 1–0.

The freezing of the River Thames drastically affected local services. The ferryboat between Greenwich and Millwall ceased to run, and local business folk were forced to make considerable detours. Most shipping came to a standstill. Old watermen recalled similar scenes of some 50 years earlier, and recounted the story of the rivermen, who in order to save a half-frozen bargee stuck in mid-stream, placed planks on the ice blocks and mounted a successful rescue.

The large quantities of snow tipped into the river by the local authorities froze into great lumps. The Thames workforce suffered considerably when they were laid off, and paraded the street with collection boxes. Local traders clubbed together and gave away quarts of soup and loaves of bread to those in need. The freezing conditions also affected the gulls, used to rich pickings. Whole flocks driven by hunger swooped down with sharpened energy on anything that offered the slightest prospect of a meal. Only the children welcomed the freezing weather because they were eager to participate in the winter sports of skating and toboganing.

In January Royal Ordnance FC were having problems, with frequent changes to the team. There were also allegations that the team was not spending sufficient time training. Peter Connolly and William Stewart were indisposed (Peter Connolly was ill and William

Stewart was getting married in Blackpool). While the team looked very smart in their all-blue outfits, results were not all that could be desired. Their position in the Southern League was as follows:

|                      | Played | Points |
|----------------------|--------|--------|
| Millwall Athletic    | 8      | 14     |
| Ilford               | 9      | 10     |
| Southampton St Mary's| 8      | 9      |
| Reading              | 9      | 9      |
| Luton Town           | 7      | 8      |
| Clapton              | 7      | 6      |
| Royal Ordnance       | 10     | 6      |
| Swindon Town         | 6      | 4      |
| Chatham              | 6      | 4      |

In the Second Division too the pressure to obtain points was starting to take its toll, and one of the worst matches ever played at the Manor Grounds was against Burton Wanderers. The attendance was 6,000, the ground was hard, and during the game there were some nasty falls.

**Woolwich Arsenal v Burton Wanderers, 26 January 1895**
The game started at a fast pace; for the first 15 minutes play was fairly even. Then from a Howat free kick, Henderson scored the first goal. Brown was unfortunate soon after, as his shot skimmed the Arsenal cross-bar. Davis then added a second goal for Arsenal, but this was disallowed because the home side had appealed against a foul just before scoring. The free kick was unproductive. This event was followed by much rough play, the half-time score being 1–0 to the Arsenal.

In the second half the game became even more unpleasant, with numerous free kicks being awarded against the visitors. The crowd was particularly upset because the referee appeared to order off a player who had been cautioned several times, then changed his mind and allowed him to stay. Just before the end of the match a penalty was awarded against the Arsenal, from which Brown scored. The final result was 1–1. When the teams were leaving the pitch, one of the Wanderers pushed O'Brien. This incensed the local crowd who was determined to get at the Burton team. The directors quickly moved the visitors into the safety of the pavilion. Mr Brodie, the referee, was at the rear of the column, when he was struck on the temple and left unconscious. Joe Powell rushed forward and threw the culprit to the ground, but the crowd assisted in the offender's escape.

A large body of police led by Inspector Goodall cleared the ground. The injured Mr Brodie was conveyed to the doctor's residence for treatment, and later recovered with a slight discoloration to one eye. He left Dr Williams' house on Monday and returned home to Wolverhampton. The Arsenal FC was given an official warning, and the Manor Grounds were suspended for six weeks.

Jimmy Hill, the former Royal Arsenal player, was disgusted with the crowd's treatment of his old colleague Jack Brodie. They had played together in Wolverhampton Wanderers' first ever FA Cup-tie winning team in 1883–4.

*Teams:*

**Arsenal:** Storer, goal; Powell and Caldwell, backs; Davis, Boyle and Howat, halfbacks; Sharpe, O'Brien, Buchanan, Crawford and Henderson, forwards.

**Burton Wanderers:** Walls, goal; Cunningham and Draper, backs; Draycott, Ward and Lowe, halfbacks; Rose, Brown, E Capes, A Capes and Garfield, forwards.

Adrian Capes (born in Burton on Trent, 1873), inside right for the Wanderers, was fortunate to be transferred to Nottingham Forest in the 1897–8 season. In the 1898 FA Cup Final, Forest beat John Goodall's Derby County 3–1. Adrian, easily recognizable by his 'baby face', scored two goals.

That season two teams in the Second Division of the Football League represented the town of Burton. As could be expected the two teams were forced to merge for financial reasons in 1901, with the new name Burton United. However, even this was not successful. The later Burton Albion Club was not in any way affiliated to the defunct Burton United.

Often at work and in the local public houses the subject would arise as to which was the better team, the new Woolwich Arsenal or the old Royal Arsenal? Naturally David Danskin would argue in favour of the latter. They were soon to find out. In April, Woolwich Arsenal were to play Royal Ordnance at their new home in Maze Hill. The professionals were nearly at full strength, while Ordnance was without their star forward Peter Connolly. While Arsenal had finished seventh of sixteen teams in their first season in the Second Division of the Football League, Ordnance had finished nearly bottom of the Southern League. The

Arsenal had drawn against Millwall in March, champions of the Southern League. So Danskin was supporting Ordnance, but would have become a little hard of hearing if anybody had suggested a wager.

**Royal Ordnance v Woolwich Arsenal, 25 April 1895**
Arsenal began very confidently, and it must be admitted that they appeared much the better team. The game soon developed into a match between the Arsenal forwards and the dour Ordnance rearguard. Nearing the end of the first half, Ordnance scored the first goal. It was a high dropping shot that Harry Storer thought was going over the bar, and much to his embarrassment went in the net.

In the second half Arsenal made far more effort but to no avail. The game finished 15 minutes early due to bad light, Ordnance winning 1–0.

Naturally the Arsenal was full of excuses! One of the worst grounds they had played upon, the pitch was too small, and so on. The Ordnance supporters were jubilant.

On 7 September 1895 a brief obituary was published in the *Fife Free Press*. 'At Balsusney Road, Kirkcaldy, on the first inst., Peter, third son of John Connolly, contractor, age 26 years 8 months – deeply regretted, RIP.'

The death of Peter Connolly was a shock and great personal loss. Peter, Jack McBean and David Danskin had always been great friends, and shared so much together. Connolly was without doubt the Royal Arsenal's greatest player, being equally brilliant as a full-back or forward. In their early games he was worth a goal start. While always unassuming he was always a good friend. His death from tuberculosis at such an early age was a tragic loss to all his family and friends.

Rugby was to follow soccer in the introduction of professionalism. At a meeting held in the George Hotel, Huddersfield on 29 August 1895, the professional Rugby League was formed.

In November 1895 Aston Villa reported the loss of the FA Cup at the Meeting of the FA Committee. It had been stolen from the shop window of W Shillock, boot and shoe manufacturer in Birmingham. A reward of £10 was offered for information leading to the recovery of the Cup, but it was never seen again. Villa was fined £25 by the FA, the cost of a new trophy.

The Danskins had always wanted a daughter, and on 22 May 1896 Sarah Georgina Janet Danskin was born. Sadly, she was weak and sickly from birth, and her short life ended when she died from bronchitis on 20 February 1897. Georgie was mentally and physically exhausted, and she and David mourned their loss for some considerable time.

For the next few years Arsenal continued to play in the Second Division of the Football League against moderate northern opposition, with low attendances. In the world outside of football, interesting changes and events were taking place.

1896 was an eventful year with interesting items of news. The Red Flag Act was repealed: cars were no longer preceded by a man carrying a red flag. The speed limit was raised from 4 to 20 mph. Doctors in Scotland began using the new X-ray machines. A new newspaper was born, the *Daily Mail*, described as 'brash and breezy'. Moving pictures were seen for the first time in London. These American films, shown at 16 frames per second, showed waves breaking on a beach, dance routines, boxing matches, athletics and the like. The Prince of Wales's colt Persimmon won the Derby, a popular result.

English businessmen, with the backing of Cecil Rhodes, unsuccessfully attempted to invade the coveted gold-rich Transvaal, a republic of South Africa held by the Boers (Dutch farmers).

In January 1897 Arsenal were unexpectedly beaten at Millwall in the third qualifying round of the FA Cup 4–2. After their humiliating defeat the Arsenal FC directors decided to appoint a professional manager, and the first to be appointed was Thomas Brown Mitchell, a Scot. Initially he signed additional players (including David Hannah who that season was joint top scorer); the results improved but unfortunately the attendances did not, and Arsenal FC was later forced to sell players including the loyal Gavin Crawford.

In 1897 Queen Victoria celebrated her Diamond Jubilee (60 years' reign), and Aston Villa won both the League Championship and the FA Cup. The Cup Final was between two evenly matched sides, with Villa narrowly beating Everton 3–2.

In September 1898, Kitchener avenged the death of General Gordon in 1885 by destroying the Sudanese army. Ten thousand warriors were killed by the British-led Egyptian army, using Maxim machine guns (built at the Woolwich Arsenal), with the loss of just 28 British troops. After the battle the Union Jack was hoisted, and three cheers was given to Queen Victoria. Kitchener was so overcome with emotion that for once he was speechless and unable to dismiss the parade.

Hiram S Maxim, an American electrical engineer, had invented the Maxim machine gun, which was modified for the British Army's use in 1891. It weighed only 40 pounds and fired 650 rounds a minute. Maxim also invented a heavier machine gun with a 1.46 inch calibre, known as the 'Pom-Pom', which could fire an explosive shell. The Boers were to use this against the British.

1899 was a marvellous year for the Danskins, as David's cousin David and his wife arrived in Woolwich. He was then 29, seven years younger than David. David and Agnes had married in 1892 in Buckhaven near Kirkcaldy. Agnes' father George Shand was a pit head manager. At home David had been a wood turner, but with his cousin's help he obtained work as an iron driller at the Woolwich Arsenal. For years David Danskin had been surrounded by hundreds of Georgina's relatives (at least it had seemed that way), and at long last he had his own kin in Woolwich, who could tell him the family gossip first hand. At first Georgie was pleased to welcome the new arrivals, but after a while David got the message that she was a bit tired of yet another welcome celebration party. In June 1899 David and Agnes' first daughter Agnes was born.

# Chapter 8

In October 1899 war broke out between the British and the Boer Republics in South Africa. At first, the 15,000 British troops were outnumbered by 50,000 Boers, and the British suffered a heavy defeat with 2,000 dead and the loss of 12 heavy guns. They retreated to await the arrival of reinforcements. When they arrived, Sir Redvers Buller, Commander-in-Chief, made a major error by splitting his inexperienced troops into three groups against battle-hardened Boer guerrillas. All three forces were defeated decisively, and Buller requested the British government's permission to surrender. This was refused. Queen Victoria commented, 'We are not interested in the possibilities of defeat, they do not exist.' The Boers then made the mistake of laying siege to Ladysmith, Kimberley and Mafeking, which tied down their forces. They were at their best when using hit and run tactics.

John Hobson, a reporter for the *Manchester Guardian*, was sent to South Africa to get a first-hand report. His assessment was:

> *We are fighting in order to place a small international oligarchy of mine owners and speculators in power at Pretoria. Englishmen will surely do well to recognise that the economic and political destinies of South Africa are, and seem likely to remain, in the hands of men most of whom are foreigners by origin, whose trade is finance, and whose trade interests are not chiefly British.*

Munitions production was stepped up, and Royal Arsenal workers went on a six-day working week. The local army garrisons were partially depleted, which in turn affected the attendance at the Manor Grounds.

In 1899 Harry Bradshaw was appointed Arsenal's third professional manager: his predecessors Thomas Mitchell and George Elcoat had each lasted only one season. It must be stressed that Arsenal's Second Division performance under each of these managers was good, considering the lack of funding.

| 1897/98 (Mitchell) | 1898/99 (Elcoat) | 1899/00 (Bradshaw) |
|---|---|---|
| Burnley 1 | Manchester City 1 | The Wednesday 1 |
| Newcastle United 2 | Glossop North End 2 | Bolton Wanderers 2 |

| Manchester City 3 | Leicester Fosse 3 | Small Heath 3 |
| Newton Heath 4 | Newton Heath 4 | Newton Heath 4 |
| Arsenal 5 | Arsenal 7 | Arsenal 8 |

Mafeking was relieved on 17 May 1900 by Brigadier General Plumer. The news reached London by a Reuters news agency dispatch on 18 May, and the whole of London celebrated. Crowds formed in the streets and sang patriotic songs, special editions of the newspapers were printed, and the Prince of Wales led the festivities at the Covent Garden Opera House, when the news was shouted from the gallery.

The small garrison of Mafeking (meaning 'a place of stones'), had been manned by 1,200 volunteers and police under the command of Colonel Baden-Powell. There was very little artillery, and many guns were improvised including the famous Wolf gun, a four and a half inch Howitzer made from a drainpipe by Major Panzera. It fired cannon-balls made at an ad hoc blast furnace. The gun was pictured on banknotes issued during the siege. The nickname 'Wolf' was given to Baden-Powell by the natives. There were 160 British casualties and the Boers had double that number. It was an insignificant tin-roofed town.

In July 1900, Baden-Powell was assigned to the evacuation of Rustenburg. Much to the annoyance of Lord Roberts, Commander in Chief, British Forces, he appeared to be unwilling to leave. Roberts wrote to Lord Lansdowne, 'Baden-Powell seems to have a strange fancy for being besieged.'

Robert Baden-Powell, born in 1857, played in goal for the school football team while at Charterhouse. He was a poor student academically, but excelled at amateur dramatics. Always enthusiastic about sport, he was later associated with Chiswick Park FC. Baden-Powell founded the Boy Scout movement in 1907.

Queen Victoria died on 22 January 1901 at Osbourne House on the Isle of Wight. She was 81. Most of her family, including the new monarch, Edward VII, were at her bedside. Britain entered a period of national mourning. Certain football teams were criticized for 'not having the decency to prevent their teams playing at a time of national mourning'. However, it was noted in the press that between 26 January and 2 February, more games of football had been played at Cambridge, Oxford and Eton in eight days than by all the professional Association and Rugby football clubs in England and Scotland combined.

There had been much talk within Arsenal for some considerable time as to whether the club should remain in the Second Division or join the Southern League. The Southern League appeared to be getting stronger following the appearance of Southampton in the 1899–1900 FA Cup Final.

In the 6 February 1901 edition of *Football Chat and Athletic World* it was reported that the half-yearly meeting of the Arsenal FC only lasted half an hour and the attendance was thin. Mr T J Bentley had given notice of the following motion, but wrote, withdrawing it:

> *That in the opinion of this meeting of shareholders, after carefully taking into consideration the very unsatisfactory state, both financially and otherwise, it would be for the best interest of the club and all concerned for the directors to apply for admission to the Southern League next season and abandon all further engagements with the English League after the present season.*

Although the idea of joining the Southern League had been mooted, Mr Bradshaw, the courteous Manager of Woolwich Arsenal, indicated when interviewed by *Football Chat* that he was not really interested in leaving the Football League because he was always optimistic that one day Arsenal would be promoted to the First Division.

In the League, Arsenal finished seventh behind Grimsby Town, Small Heath and Burnley, and Tottenham Hotspur won the FA Cup, beating Sheffield United. The venue for the FA Cup was Crystal Palace, with an estimated attendance of over 110,000. Spurs, from the Southern League, started favourites. Priest for Sheffield scored the first goal after approximately 20 minutes, and a few minutes later, Brown headed the equalizer. No further goals were scored and the replay took place at Bolton.

The gate for the replay of approximately 35,000 was disappointing. Contrary to popular opinion Spurs played much better in the north than expected. At half-time the Blades led one goal to nil but in the second half the Spurs came back strongly with goals from Cameron, Smith and Brown to win the cup 3–1. Fatty Foulke must have had an off-day.

David Danskin was finding the pressure of work (because of the demands of the Boar War) very stressful. The six-day week had destroyed his weekend football aspirations. For some years he had toyed with the idea of self-employment. As an engineer he needed to be associated with a growth mechanical industry. The cycle trade fitted this criterion.

As with most new inventions, the only people who could afford the early cycles were the wealthy. They could be seen regularly riding their cycles, dressed in the height of fashion in the London parks. The first all-metal high bicycle commercially produced in quantity was the 'Ariel' manufactured at the St Agnes Works, Coventry, by Smith & Starley in the 1870s. The models had progressed from the early high boneshakers, normally with the pedals in the wheel, and solid India-rubber seven-eighths tyres. In 1889 low chain-driven safety bicycles were produced commercially with pneumatic (air-filled) tyres. The first Dunlop pneumatic tyres were glued onto the rim of the wheels. In the 1890s a Frenchman named Michelin produced the first detachable tyre.

By the late 1890s the demand for cycles amongst the upper class had begun to wane, and the average cost fell from £20 to around £12. This made the cycle a more affordable proposition for the working class. Women especially were drawn to this new leisure pursuit, which provided them with a new freedom to travel further afield.

In 1901 the Danskins purchased a freehold shop, with the assistance of a bank loan, in Herbert Road, Woolwich. On the first floor was their living accommodation, consisting of a large parlour with a bay window and a rear bedroom. On the ground floor was a good sized showroom, with a kitchen and toilet behind. To the back of this they built an extension, which they used as a production factory. Best of all they erected a small greenhouse, which was David's pride and joy. The business basically made cycle frames, and assembled parts and accessories purchased from the Midlands. Two of the main suppliers were BSA, which had a ten-acre factory site in Birmingham, and Raleigh, with nearly eight acres of factory in Nottingham.

By 1901 the price of a standard bicycle had fallen to approximately £9, still too costly for the average working man. To stay in business the Danskins had to find various ways of creating sales. This was done by allowing trade-ins on old cycles (vintage cycles were updated where possible and resold).

Not everybody adjusted easily from riding the early high cycles to the new machines. Bill Julian, a keen cyclist, told David of his friend George Beale's experience at Boston. George was used to riding a Penny-farthing with a small rear wheel. He had purchased a new Rover Safety Cycle. George jumped off behind as normal, so the lower part of his body made violent contact with the top of the wheel. This resulted in a very serious internal injury. Two local doctors performed a painful but successful operation the following day.

A savings club allowed people to put a little by every week until they had enough money to buy a bicycle. The Danskins also encouraged clubs to purchase their machines. One or two bicycles could be purchased, and added to when funds became available. Repair work also generated a good deal of business.

5 April 1902 was the date of the Ibrox Park disaster. This was the venue for the Scotland–England match. Officially the stadium held 80,000, but on that fateful day in April the number was thought to be nearer 100,000. The sway of the crowd was believed to have opened up a large section of the wooden terrace, and hundreds of spectators plunged through the gap. Sadly the police thought part of the crowd had rioted, and rode into the mayhem. Twenty-five spectators lost their lives. Surprisingly enough many of the spectators were unaware of the catastrophe until returning home and reading the newspapers. All credit to Rangers, they made every effort to compensate the victims' families financially.

David Danskin's former shop

In South Africa the British built concentration camps and interned nearly a quarter of the Boer population. The internees were women and children (the men were shot). Over 22,000 children died from exposure, starvation and typhus. The Boer War ended in May 1902 with the signing of the treaty of Vereeniging. The terms included substantial compensation for the reinstatement of Boer property, and the promise of self-government for the Orange Free State and Transvaal. (This was granted in 1907.) After the war Lord Kitchener went amongst the Boers shaking their hands, saying, 'We are all friends now.' Not all the Boers were so conciliatory. The war cost Britain over £200 million and over 50,000 casualties. Huge crowds greeted the returning troops.

The end of the war affected Woolwich Arsenal factory workers. They returned to a five and a half day week and over 2,000 workers were dismissed, with the threat of further redundancies in the future.

Whilst this bad news did not help the domestic side of David Danskin's business, thankfully the commercial side was growing. The local tradesmen realized the benefits of being able to deliver goods by tricycles and bicycles with large boxes attached to the front. This in turn led to the demise of the horse and cart.

On 20 November 1902 Nellie and Fred Beardsley were both excited and proud to announce the birth of their daughter Doris. They had been childless since the death of poor Fred junior in 1889. To them it was a minor miracle as Nellie was then 46.

West Bromwich Albion and Preston North End had been demoted from the First Division in 1900–1. In the following season, 1901–2, West Bromwich became Second Division champions, with Preston finishing third. Woolwich Arsenal finished fourth, their highest ever league position. Fatty Foulke's team Sheffield United beat Southampton 2–1 in the FA Cup after a replay.

Following the redundancies, and rumours of more to come, there was much dissatisfaction amongst the Arsenal workers. The Amalgamated Society of Engineers, the most powerful and militant union at the works, was together with other unions affiliated to the Woolwich Independent Labour Party. In December 1902 Will Crooks was invited to become the prospective Labour candidate for Woolwich. At the age of nine he had been an apprentice cooper. Crooks had become a member of the London County Council in 1892 and Mayor of Poplar in 1901. He was politically a moderate. Amongst Crooks' many leading supporters were Danskin's former teammates Jack Sheppard of the Co-op and Jack Humble of the Radical Clubs.

In February 1903 Lord Charles Beresford resigned from the Woolwich seat to take up other duties and a by-election was called. The Tory candidate was Geoffrey Drage. One of the major issues in the by-election was that Drage had previously voted in the House of Commons against Arsenal workers' wages being raised. His justification was that 'half a loaf was better than none'! Will Crooks promised the Woolwich Arsenal workers that if elected, he would support a rise from the then £1 1s minimum weekly wage, and fight against further redundancies. Crooks possessed a good sense of humour and was very popular with the Woolwich workers, but not so it would appear with the editor of the *Kentish Mercury*, who wrote on 6 March, 'We have too much faith in the intelligent, close reasoning men of Woolwich to believe that they are prepared to allow themselves to be captured by Mr Crooks and his promises.'

The result of the by-election was Crooks 8,687 votes; Drage 5,458 votes. Crooks became the first Labour member for Woolwich and the fourth member of the Parliamentary Labour Representation Committee in the House of Commons. The editorial in the *Kentish Mercury* on 13 March stated, 'Those who know the circumstances as they are, are not surprised that Mr Crooks succeeds Lord Charles Beresford, but it is nevertheless remarkable that the voting in his favour should have been so considerable.' Labour was to make further gains locally in the Borough Council and London County Council elections.

Shortly after 8 am on 18 June 1903, 16 men were killed and 14 injured in an explosion at a cordite factory on Plumstead marshes. A team of men had filled a 9.2 shell weighing 453 lb with 46 lb of lyddite and were about to place it in the drying oven when it exploded with terrible force. As soon as news of the disaster spread, crowds from all parts of the borough flocked to the Arsenal gates. A list of the dead and injured was posted and was eagerly scanned by relatives of the men employed in the danger buildings. Four names of men injured were listed in error and had to be removed. There were distressing scenes when the wives and family of the dead arrived at midday and were allowed to visit the mortuary. Trade was paralyzed and the one topic of conversation was the scale of the accident and awful fate of the men.

Expressions of sympathy and regret came flooding in from all over the borough, and included the hands at the factory, the Mayor of Greenwich in a telegram to the Mayor of Woolwich, Woolwich Borough Council and Arsenal FC. The Secretary of State for War, in informing the House, expressed regret for the occurrence, and

Questions were asked in Parliament. Mr Crooks, Labour MP for Woolwich, asked the Secretary of State whether he would refer to the Committee of Enquiry into the explosion, whether the system of payment partly by piece work, and partly by day-work rate, was a source of danger owing to the desire to obtain extra pay over the day-rate wages. He was given an undertaking that the system of payment would be reviewed.

The excessive loss of life and injury was also attributed to the fact that the Royal Arsenal was not subject to Home Office regulations in the same way as private firms. Far too many men were employed in one building, the quantity of explosives stored was too large, and the danger buildings were either too close together or insufficiently mounded. It was considered that these conditions would be considerably improved if the Royal Arsenal was placed under the regulations.

Woolwich Arsenal FC was to improve yet again in the 1902–3 season by finishing third behind Manchester City and Small Heath. Bury were to beat Derby 6–0 in the FA Cup. One of Bury's FA Cup winning team was fullback J McEwan, known as 'Punch'. In 1913 he became an Arsenal trainer. Known for his cheerful disposition, he remained with Arsenal for many years.

For Arsenal, success bred success. Bradshaw had achieved the impossible by improving the results with very limited means. This in turn increased the attendances, and with the extra income he was able to purchase better-quality players. In the 1903–4 season Woolwich Arsenal were runners-up to Preston North End. Both teams were promoted to the First Division of the Football League. Having won Woolwich Arsenal promotion, Bradshaw promptly resigned to take up a more lucrative appointment with Fulham FC. His successor was the former Hibernian manager Phil Kelso.

In 1905 Middlesbrough were to cause an outcry when they purchased Alf Common, a rugged, quick, goalscoring forward, from Sunderland for a record £1,000. While playing with Sheffield United he had another occupation outside soccer, and received two wages. John Nicholson, the long-serving secretary/manager of Sheffield United, suggested that Alf save half the money from his football wages and he would look after it for him.

When Alf later returned to his native Sunderland he saw a particular house for sale and asked John Nicholson to buy it for him. A few days later he spoke to his father, 'I see they are selling this house.' His father replied, 'Yes it was sold yesterday. I wonder if we shall have to go?' 'You won't have to Dad, I have bought it.' His parents were over-joyed: they had lived in the house for 30 years.

Alf Common was renowned for his practical jokes. One must sympathize with the Sheffield United team when both Alf and Fatty Foulke were teammates there. Like Billy Foulke, Alf had a weight problem. Although his height was 5 ft 8 in, he weighed 13 stone. They were both awarded FA Cup winners' medals in 1902. In 1910 Alf was to join Woolwich Arsenal.

In August 1906 the weather was good with plenty of sunshine, little rain, and a fairly constant warm temperature. On 30 August the temperature reached 89.1 °F (31.7 °C) in Berkshire. In early September most areas in Britain were recording temperatures of 90–95 °F. The heat, combined with poor sanitation, caused a fivefold increase in gastro-intestinal infant deaths. There were many cases of heat-stroke among manual workers, and the Woolwich Arsenal, like many other factories, was forced on some days to allow its workers to have the afternoon off.

Although the majority of the working class were dedicated to their cycles, there was a growing movement amongst the affluent towards the motor car. By 1906 there were more than 30,000 cars on the road, and the numbers were increasing. That year King Edward had driven at 60 mph on the Brighton Road (the speed limit was still 20 mph). The expanding employment area was the Midlands. It had commenced with the cycle industry, and the new companies like BSA, Rudge-Whitworth, Triumph and Royal Enfield then diversified into motor bikes and motor cars.

The Woolwich district had been in a state of decline since the Boer War. The government was determined to reduce the Woolwich Arsenal's staffing from the original level of over 13,000 to approximately 5,000.

One effect of these factors was that the Danskins had to make some hard business decisions, which included a possible move to the Midlands. Georgie was at first against the move, because of family ties. Her mother was now 76 and she wondered whether she would see her again. Her two nephews George and Jonathan, both bakers, had married in recent years. On the other hand her and David's son, 13-year-old Billy, now assisting David in the workshop, was keen to move. The cycle shop had been a profitable business, but the Danskins relied heavily on the Arsenal workers for their living.

Billy would miss his Saturday job of selling Arsenal FC programmes, for which he received one penny for each dozen sold. After the match he and the other boys sold the '*Pink un*', a pink football edition of the *Star*, which sold for a halfpenny. After selling 25, they were paid two and a half pence commission.

In January 1907 the Danskins sold their business to a Mr Goodman for £550 and moved to Coventry. They chose Coventry because a new private ordnance works had been opened. The factory site was built in 1897 by Thomas Smith for maintenance and development of the Dreadnought battleship. In 1901 the 60-acre factory had been transferred to the Coventry Ordnance Works Ltd, which combined three companies: John Brown, Cammell Laird and Fairfield of Govan. Naturally they would welcome experienced engineers, and although David had no wish to work in ordnance again, he felt that if he failed to obtain work in the fledgling motor industry, he had something in reserve.

On 23 May 1907 he commenced work at the Standard car factory as an examiner. The company had been founded in 1903 by an engineer called Reginald Maudsley. Maudsley's family originally produced marine engines in the Lambeth area. Reginald Maudsley, in conjunction with Sir John Wolfe Barry, was to become involved in various projects (prior to founding the car company), including the construction of the Barry Docks near Cardiff. A few months before David's arrival, Charles Friswell became Chairman. Friswell was sales-oriented and a good communicator, although some said a little too flamboyant. While the company's products were popular (and additional staff including David were engaged, bringing the staff levels to 100 plus), the business had good growth potential, and like many small companies, it survived with the assistance of its bankers. The company produced both six and four cylinder cars.

Soon after David commenced work at Standard Cars, the Danskins purchased a new house in North Street, Coventry, with the proceeds of their cycle business. Georgie was over the moon. The property was a small two-bedroomed, bay-fronted, semi-detached house, with a front parlour and a large rear living room. Georgie's pride and joy was the downstairs bathroom. David made sure the rear garden was south facing, as naturally this was important for his greenhouse. Conveniently located a few doors away was the Rose and Woodbine public house.

On 3 March 1910 David's father died of pneumonia at Leslie in Fifeshire. Sadly, he had been a paraplegic for two years. In April the same year, David heard from old colleagues that the original Woolwich Arsenal FC had gone into liquidation. Arsenal had been secure as long they were winning. Poor results exposed the problems of access to Plumstead. Although the Manor Grounds were adjacent to Plumstead Station, it was a difficult journey from Cannon Street or London Bridge. Growing competition from London clubs such as Chelsea, Spurs, Fulham and Clapton Orient gave football enthusiasts plenty of choice closer to home. Arsenal was in a downward spiral. They had to sell star players when gates fell. This resulted in even lower attendances.

The hopes and aspirations of the Arsenal workers had failed to materialize. The liquidator, Mr Brannan, sold the original club, grounds and so on to a group of local businessmen, including George Leavey, who had assisted the former club by occasionally paying outstanding debts out of his own pocket.

The new company shares were offered to the general public in May. There was a change in the status of the new shareholders. The bulk of the new shareholders were small businessmen, publicans, builders, printers, accountants and the like. The Nottingham men, including Fred Beardsley, had not subscribed. The major new shareholders were Henry Norris (Mayor of Fulham and Chairman of Fulham FC), with 240 shares, William Hall with 240 shares, George Leavey with 100 shares, and a surprise shareholder, Tottenham Hotspur FC, with 100 shares (which they sold on 26 July 1910). Smaller shareholders of interest were Richard Horsington, now a publican, with five shares, William Crooks with five shares, and Jack Humble with one share. There were only five other Arsenal workers who purchased one share each, out of a total of 1,280 shares. This effectively gave Henry Norris and his friend William Hall, with 37.5 per cent of the shares, control of the new company.

In August 1912 Georgie was very upset to hear that her 80-year-old mother, Sarah Harradon, had died, but it must have been a relief for the Fletchers as she had been becoming more and more forgetful.

During April 1913 it was with some personal sadness that David was to hear that Arsenal had played their last game at the Manor Grounds. For him this was the end of an era. The move had been planned for some time. Arsenal FC at the end of the 1912–13 season had been relegated from the First Division.

On a more cheerful note, David was proud when his son Billy, then 22, joined him at Standard Motors as an examiner. His pay was approximately £2 per week, based on a 45-hour week.

Great interest that year was generated by Lord Baden-Powell's wedding present, a six-cylinder Standard Landaulette, which had been donated by the Boy Scouts movement. The boys had subscribed a maximum of one penny each, and the scout masters were limited to one shilling each. Baden-Powell's wife was in her twenties, and later assisted him with the Girl Guides.

In September 1913 the Arsenal opened their new ground at Highbury, which was a huge gamble and badly mistimed, as the country went to war in 1914. Fortunately Billy was not conscripted because most of the car factories switched to the production of armaments, which were essential services.

On 30 March 1916 tragedy struck. After a long illness David's dear wife Georgina died of emphysema. Sadly she did not live to see the marriage of her son Billy to Mary Jones, a watchmaker's daughter, in June. 1916 was not only a bad year for David but also a disastrous one for the British Army. On 1 July 19,000 men were killed and 57,000 injured in one day at the Somme.

In 1918 the war ended, and David became a grandfather. His first grandson was named Geoffrey. As a chief examiner his work kept him very busy, but living on his own, he felt lonely on occasions. On 12 May that year he married Rose Richardson, who was one of his inspection team. He was then 55 and Rose was 27. In the period after the First World War it was not uncommon for men to be quite a bit older than their wives. He felt sure Georgina would have approved of the marriage, and added her name to his own on the marriage certificate, calling himself David 'George' Danskin.

His new marriage to Rose was happy and fruitful. They were blessed with three healthy bairns, Rose (called Hilda), Ellen and Richard, born in 1919, 1920 and 1926. David's second grandson Neville was born in 1924.

Billy was as wild as ever. After joining various companies he became an employee of Rudge-Whitworth, a motor cycle firm. In 1922 they entered a team of ten machines in the Isle of Man TT races. From a business point of view, the experience was a total failure: only one bike finished, taking 14th place. According to Billy, the only memorable event was a night out with seven colleagues. They all rode on one motorbike and were chased by the local police, who unbelievably failed to catch them.

# Chapter 9

In 1936, at the age of 73, David Danskin was in Coventry Municipal Hospital after aggravating an old football injury to his leg. He had fallen awkwardly when trying to catch a tram.

1936 was of course the year that Arsenal was to play Sheffield United at Wembley in the FA Cup Final. The game was to be played on the coming Saturday. Fortunately the matron allowed David to use a radio on the ward.

This was an interesting match between a veteran Arsenal team and a younger Second Division side. In fact four of the Arsenal team had played in the 1930 Cup Final. There would have been five but Roberts was not available on the day. Arsenal's key player was Ted Drake, the former Southampton striker. The team had recently been missing his strike rate in front of goal. Ted had only just recovered from a cartilage operation. He had played the previous Saturday in a league match, and had scored the winning goal, but there was doubt whether he would survive 90 minutes on the lush Wembley turf. This was a decision that Arsenal manager George Allison had to make.

Many pundits predicted that one of the key elements in the match would be the duel between veteran Herbie Roberts, the Arsenal centre half, and Jock Dodds, the United centre forward. Dodds had scored 34 goals in the league that season.

Arsenal appeared to have lost their touch. They had been League champions three years in a row, but in 1936 they looked like they would finish sixth.

The programme began at 2.30 pm with community singing, and the match started at 3.00 pm. Just before 2.30 pm David sat in a chair frantically trying to tune in the radio. After much crackling he found the right signal and turned the sound up slightly.

'Good afternoon, everybody. Today as you know is Cup Final day. Our commentators are our own Ivan Sharpe and football expert F N S Creek.'

'Good afternoon, listeners. Welcome to Wembley. My name is Ivan Sharpe and my fellow commentator today is the well-known former England international footballer and author of *A History of the Corinthian Football Club*, F N S Creek. Norman, thank you for being with us this afternoon.'

'My pleasure, Ivan.'

'No doubt, listeners, you can hear the community singing in the background. The conductor is the popular T P Ratcliff of the *News Chronicle*, accompanied by His Majesty's Welsh Guards.'

[The crowd sang *Pack up your troubles in your old kit bag*, followed by *Abide with me, On Ilkley Moor baht 'at, My girl's a Yorkshire girl, Annie Laurie, Land of hope and glory, Love's old sweet song*, and finally *Danny Boy*. The patients on David's ward joined in quietly.]

'Tell me, Norman, has the game changed much since you played for the Corinthians?'

'Yes. The Corinthians used to play with five forwards in a straight line. Now usually two of the forwards drop back, forming a 'W' formation, and of course the former centre halfback plays deep as a centre fullback.'

'How has that affected the game?'

'It's made it much faster.'

'Just before the players come onto the pitch, perhaps you can run through the team lists for us, Norman.'

'Certainly.' Norman quickly read out the details for Sheffield United. 'Their goalkeeper is Jack Smith, a local Sheffield lad, left back Charlie Wilkinson, who has such a good understanding with Harry Hooper, the right back and captain. Centre half is Tom Johnson, from the famous football family. It's a big week for Tom, as I expect our listeners know: he was married on Thursday. He and his new wife Gwen will have to wait until after the match for their honeymoon. Left half Archie McPherson is a former inside left with Glasgow Rangers. Right half Ernest Jackson is another local lad. Outside left Bert Williams, a Welsh international. Inside left Jack Pickering, another local, who is an accountant and plays part-time. Centre forward Jock Dodds, a prolific goal scorer. Inside right Bob Barclay, an influential member of the squad, and England international. Outside right, Harold Barton, possesses good pace and a powerful shot.

'Arsenal's goalkeeper is Alec Wilson, a Scot, who replaced the injured Frank Moss, very athletic. Left back Eddie Hopgood, the well-known England international. Right back George Male, the England fullback. Centre half Herbie Roberts, who was injured when Arsenal won the cup in 1930. Left half Wilf Copping, ex miner, England international. Right half Jack Crayston, another England international and a great tennis player. Outside left Cliff Bastin, the famous England international. Inside left Alec James, captain of

Arsenal, a Scottish international. Centre forward Ted Drake, England international, a quick strong intelligent player, who has hopefully recovered from his operation. Inside right Ray Bowden, England international, who played centre forward when Ted Drake was injured. Outside right Joe Hulme, England international, who plays cricket for Middlesex, playing in his fourth Cup Final for Arsenal. The referee this afternoon is the distinguished Harry Nattrass.'

'Well timed, Norman: the players are now coming on to the pitch. United in their red and white striped shirts and black shorts, and Arsenal wearing red shirts with white sleeves and white shorts. I notice that Ted Drake is wearing a very large bandage on one leg. That looks a bad sign. The team captains and the referee are together in the centre circle. Arsenal wins the toss and United prepare to kick off for the 1936 Cup Final.'

'Dodds pushes the ball through to Barton on the wing. He passes to Barclay – it's all United. Brilliant back heel from Barclay to Pickering who shoots too high.' [There were groans from the crowd.] 'Wilson takes the goal kick that nearly reaches the halfway line. United are away again, a quick through ball to Barton who centres, Dodds and Barclay going in, Wilson's caught the ball – no he hasn't, he's dropped it at the feet of Barclay – it must be – [ooh] – amazing, Wilson's recovered, I don't believe it. He dropped the ball, Barclay looked like he must score and somehow Wilson vindicated himself by making an amazing split-second save by hurling himself sideways to snatch the ball. Barclay I believe should have scored – Hopgood taking the ball away now for the Arsenal – I believe Bob Barclay will kick himself later. If he had followed through he must have scored.'

\* \* \*

'It's a quick pass from James who is playing from a deep position to Bastin on the left. He gives a very quick centre but Johnson clears. We have seen great fighting spirit from United, but as expected the Arsenal defence has held firm. There is a great chance here for Dodds.' [Groans.] 'Oh, he just hesitated for a split-second. That was just enough time for Male to intercept the ball and make a long clearance to Bowden, who touches the ball to Hulme on the right wing. He's having an outstanding game.'

\* \* \*

'Drake's going through – offside. That's the first time Drake touched the ball and he runs into an offside position. So far play has been pretty even.'

\* \* \*

'Free kick in a dangerous position for a foul on Pickering. Hooper about to take it.' [Groans.] 'Hooper's blasted it wide. So far the Arsenal halfbacks have been creating chances by sending long through balls to the wingers. They in turn, especially Hulme, have been feeding the inside forward but unfortunately Drake seems to have lost some of his impetus. For Sheffield – there's a nice move here by James – Jackson clears – for Sheffield without doubt the right wing of Barclay and Barton are having the most impact.'

\* \* \*

'It's a pass back to Hooper, he's missed, Barton like lightning is in, he's pushed the ball to either Drake or Bowden.' [Ooh, groan.] 'Bowden pounced, only to miss an open goal. He'll remember that miss for years to come.'

\* \* \*

'Both sides are now using their wingers well – Wilson looks like he's now recovered his nerve – a nice ball from James to Hulme – again the build-up is wasted. The United defence is playing well, but my feeling is Drake is playing too deep, and Arsenal are depending too much on Bowden in front of goal. They seem to rely too much on the long-distance shooting. Sheffield are playing a tighter game, but at times tend to be a bit too clever. So far Male and Hopgood have contained their attacks. Roberts appears so far to be winning the duel with Dodds, but Dodds did once hit the cross-bar.'

'Harry Nattrass has blown for half-time.'

\* \* \*

'Quite an eventful first half. Perhaps you would like to give our listeners your expert opinion of the first half, Norman?'

'Thank you, Ivan. Well I thought....'

[There was much anticipation in the ward, but David was having difficulty in containing his excitement so he did not disturb the other patients. Thankfully the tea trolley came around about the same time as the interval in the match.]

The football commentary continued.

'It's Arsenal to kick off. Drake gives a short side pass to James. Crayston meantime has raced into the United half. James is cleverly taking the ball forward. He releases a long pinpoint pass to Crayston, who is still running into a position behind United's centre half Johnson. Crayston is approximately 20 yards from the penalty area. Hooper is about to tackle. Crayston quickly dribbles past, feints with his right foot, and then hits a vicious shot towards the far post'.

[Ooh!] 'Smith makes a brilliant save.' [Loud applause.] 'That was a well rehearsed move, Norman!'

'Without a doubt, Ivan.'

Ivan continued, 'I think Smith is an outstanding goalkeeper. I really thought that Crayston was going to score!'

\* \* \*

'Yet another fine save from Smith. If the Arsenal keep this up they must score. There's now continual pressure on the United's goal. I don't think it looks too good for United at the moment, as both Jackson and Hooper appear to be limping. Hopefully it's cramp, and they might recover. All the United defence have been magnificent, especially Smith. Again the Arsenal defence return the ball into the United end.'

\* \* \*

'Arsenal on the attack, again James with the ball, he's always tricky. A quick pass to Bastin who immediately centres the ball to Drake, who's moving like a rocket into the penalty area. Drake feints one way and, G – O – A – L.' [Pandemonium broke out at the Wembley Stadium.]

David and the other patients went wild. He was to sleep well that night, and dream he scored that winning Arsenal goal.

# Appendix: Football rules, from the *Boys Own Book*, 1889

## The Open Game

The matches usually consist of eleven on either side, but this number may be increased at pleasure. A captain is chosen on each side, who directs the game for his fellows. One player always remains at the goal to defend it, by kicking back the ball to prevent it going through. The ball is kicked off from the middle of the ground. Then all players follow, but every player must keep on his right side of the ball: that is, he must not be nearer to the goal he is trying to force it through than the ball. There is no cross-bar, and the ball may be kicked to any height, so that it does not pass beyond the space, on either side, which is indicated by the goal-sticks. When the ball is kicked into the air, any player may catch it: and then, if he succeed and call out 'Three yards' he is allowed to take a run of that distance, and dropping to the ground, kick it without being interfered with by the others. The ball flies rapidly over the ground, and when it goes out at the sidelines, or the goal lines, it is kicked straight in again. *No hacking or kicking at each other with heel or toe is allowed*, neither is it allowable for one player to strike or push another. But in the open game, 'charging' is admitted. This 'charging' consists of one player butting at another with his shoulder. At Rugby the players are allowed to take up the ball, and wrestle for its possession. The side that succeeds in fairly kicking the ball through the enemy's goal wins the game.

This is the Open game, which is harmless enough, though by no means devoid of amusement. We will now see how the game is played at Eton, where much rougher exercise is allowed.

## The Close Game

As at Harrow, one player remains to defend each goal; but two act as 'corners'. Then the four strongest boys close up in a line, bending down shoulder to shoulder, with their hands on their knees; four others stand in a similar way behind them, and help to push them forward. On the other side the players do the same, and the two lines stand close together, making a sort of bridge of their shoulders. One of the 'corners' puts the ball in the centre, between the feet of these players. They then begin to push, kick and struggle, till one side bears the other down and forces the ball through the goal. Every time the ball goes out of the ground, this replacing and struggling is repeated. Players called 'bullies' are appointed to bring back the ball to the centre. Players are allowed to kick each other's shins, but this should by no means be encouraged, as the game so played becomes dangerous and brutal. Catching is not allowed; but the hands may be used to stop the ball. When it is kicked beyond the goal line a spirited race to touch it ensues, and if two players are close together, they charge each other with their shoulders, each trying to get the advantage of his adversary; whereupon a third player often comes in, and 'touches it down'. If the ball is touched in this way by a defender of the goal, it is brought to the line and kicked straight out again; but if a player of the other side touches, an exciting scene ensues. The ball is placed in front of the space marked out by the goal-sticks; then a rally, in which all the players take part, is formed. But instead of forming in two lines as before, each side makes a semicircle, so that there is no escape for the ball. Then, shoulder to shoulder, they all push and struggle till the weakest side gives way, and, falling backwards, the whole go down together in a confused heap, with the ball beneath them. They go on with the battle on the ground and struggle for the possession of the ball, in spite of mud or stones, till one or the other side 'scores a goal' by kicking the ball through the goal-sticks. But if, as often happens, no goal is gained during the match, or an equal number or goals is won on either side, then the players who obtain the most *rouges* – that is, oftenest touch the ball beyond the touch-lines on their opponents' side of the centre line – win the game.

All the games of Football are modifications of these two ways of playing; but lately the Football Association agreed to a set of rules whereby the game may be played in a uniform way at all places. The following are the revised (Association) rules.

## Laws of the Game

**I.** The limits of the ground shall be – maximum length, 200 yards, minimum length, 100 yards; maximum breadth, 200 yards; minimum breadth, 50 yards. The length and breadth shall be marked off with flags and touchline; and the goals shall be upright posts, 8 yards apart, with a bar across them, 8 feet from the ground. The average circumference of the Association Ball shall be not less than 27 inches and not more than 28 inches.

II. The winners of the toss shall have the option of kick-off or choice of goals. The game shall be commenced by a place-kick from the centre of the ground in the direction of the opposite goal line; the other side shall not approach within ten yards of the ball until it is kicked off, nor shall any player on either side pass the centre of the ground in the direction of his opponents' goal until the ball is kicked off.

III. Ends shall only be changed at half-time. After a goal is won the losing side shall kick-off, but after the change of ends at half-time, the ball shall be kicked off by the opposite side from that which originally did so; and always as provided in Law II.

IV. A goal shall be won when the ball has passed between the goal posts under the bar, not being thrown, knocked, or carried by any one of the attacking sides. The ball hitting the goal or boundary posts, or goal-bar, and rebounding into play, is considered in play.

V. When the ball is in touch, a player of the opposite side to that which kicked it out shall throw it from the point on the boundary line where it left the ground. The thrower, facing the field of play, shall hold the ball above his head, and throw it with both hands in any direction, and it shall be in play when thrown in. The player throwing it in shall not play it until it has been played by another player.

VI. When a player kicks the ball, or throws it in from touch, any one of the same side who at such moment of kicking or throwing is nearer to the opponents' goal line is out of play, and may not touch the ball himself, nor in any way whatever prevent any other player from doing so, until the ball has been played, unless there are at such moment of kicking or throwing at least three of his opponents nearer their own goal line, but no player is out of play in the case of a corner kick, or when the ball is kicked from the goal line or when it has been last played by an opponent.

VII. When the ball is kicked behind the goal line by one of the opposite side, it shall be kicked off by any one of the players behind whose goal line it went, within six yards of the nearest goal post; but if kicked behind by any one of the side whose goal line it is, a player of the opposite side shall kick it from within one yard of the nearest corner flag-post. In either case no other player shall be allowed within six yards of the ball until it is kicked off.

VIII. No player shall carry, knock on, or handle the ball under any pretence whatever, except in the case of the goalkeeper who shall be allowed to use his hands in defence of his goal, either by knocking on or throwing, but not carrying the ball. The goalkeeper may be changed during the game, but not more than one player shall act as goalkeeper at the same time, and no second player shall step in and act during any period in which the regular goalkeeper may have vacated his position.

**IX.** In no case shall a goal be scored from any free kick, nor shall the ball be again played by the kicker until it has been played by another player. The kick-off and corner-flag kick shall be free kicks within the meaning of this rule.

**X.** Neither tripping, hacking nor jumping at a player shall be allowed, and no player shall use his hands to hold or push his adversary, nor charge him from behind. A player with his back towards the opponents' goal cannot claim the protection of this rule when charged behind, provided in the opinion of the umpires or referee he, in that position, is wilfully impeding his opponent.

**XI.** No player shall wear any nails, except such as have their heads driven in flush with the leather or iron plates, or gutta-percha, on the soles or heels of his boots, or on his shin guards. Any player discovered infringing this rule shall be prohibited from taking further part in the game.

**XII.** In the event of any infringement of Rules V., VI., VIII., IX., or X., a free kick shall be forfeited to the opposite side from the spot where the infringement took place.

**XIII.** In the event of an appeal for any supposed infringement of the rules, the ball shall be in play until a decision has been given.

**XIV.** Each of the competing clubs shall be entitled to appoint an umpire, whose duty it shall be to decide in all disputed points when appealed to; and by mutual arrangement a referee may be chosen to decide in all cases of difference between the umpires.

**XV.** The referee shall have power to stop the game in the event of the spectators interfering with the game.

### Definition of Terms

**A Place Kick** is a kick at the ball while it is on the ground, in any position in which the kicker may chose to place it.

**A Free Kick** is a kick at the ball in any way the kicker pleases, when it is lying on the ground; none of the kicker's opponents being allowed within six yards of the ball, but in no case can a player be forced to stand behind his own goal line.

**Hacking** is kicking an adversary intentionally.

**Tripping** is throwing an adversary by the use of the legs, or by stooping in front of him.

**Knocking on** is when a player strikes or propels the ball with his hands or arms.

**Holding** includes the obstruction of a player by the hand or any part of the arm extended from the body.

**Handling** is understood to be playing the ball with the hand or arm.

**Touch** is that part of the field, on either side of the ground, which is beyond the line of the flags.

**Carrying** is taking more that two steps when holding the ball.

### Rugby Rules – extract

**XLIX.** That unless Umpires be appointed, the Captains of the respective sides shall be the sole arbiters of all disputes, and their decisions shall be final. If the Captain of either side challenge the construction placed upon any rule, he shall have the right of appeal to the Rugby Union Committee.  ·

### Concluding Remarks

With regard to dress and style of play, we need only say that the former should be light and easy, without braces; and that perfection in the latter can only be acquired by practice. Smartness and activity are essential to good play: and, above all, it is absolutely necessary that every payer should *keep his temper.*

In *Tom Brown's Schooldays* the game, as played at Rugby, is minutely described.

## Rules of the Turton Football Club, Published 1873

The rules of Turton FC (a Lancashire club) published in 1873 were very similar to the rules of the 'open game' although they were more explicit, e.g. the goals are 12 ft wide and the distance between etc.

**2.** The Bases are 12 ft wide, and the distance between them must not exceed 150 yards. The width of the ground must not be more than 100 yards.

**10.** After a Base has been obtained, or when half-time has elapsed (supposing no Base has been previously obtained), the two sides change their respective bases.

**14.** In the case of 'Try at Goal,' two players shall be chosen, one on each side, to stand behind the kicker. Their decision shall determine whether a goal has been obtained.

# Biographies

### Humphrey Barbour 1865–1932

On 19 June 1932 (just before midnight), Humphrey Barbour was knocked down and killed by a motorcycle combination in Streatham High Road. He was returning home from the British Legion Club, where he had spent the evening. His wife Alice commented at the inquest that the road was badly lit after 11 pm. The jury returned a verdict of accidental death.

### Joseph 'Morris' Bates 1864–1905

Morris continued his career at the Woolwich Arsenal Factory, producing Maxim machine guns. In 1905 he died of phthisis pulmonalis (tuberculosis) aged 41.

### Frederick William Beardsley 1856–1939

When Arsenal FC went to Highbury, Fred joined the committee at Charlton FC. He then became disillusioned with Charlton because of their very defensive team play. Fred decided to concentrate on his sweet shop/tobacconist business in Nile Street, later Ferry Approach. He also owned a tenanted house in Coxwell Road. He died in 1939 aged 82. In 1940 a bomb demolished his former shop.

### Edmund Bee 1868–1912

One of Arsenal's first professional footballers. When his football career was over he returned to Woolwich with his locally born wife Elizabeth and resumed his old trade as a bricklayer. He died in 1912 aged 44.

### Arthur Brown 1858–1933

Long-time player and director of Royal/Woolwich Arsenal. Arthur (Nottingham born) lived at 30 Miriam Road, Plumstead, for over 40 years. He died at St Nicholas Hospital in 1933 aged 75.

### Robert W Buist 1869–1944

Bobby was later to play for Royal Ordnance. He remained an Arsenal factory worker until his retirement, and died in Plumstead aged 74. Brother of George Buist.

### James Charteris 1867–1895

After his football injury, he returned to Motherwell, where in early 1895 he became seriously ill and died on the morning of 17 May, age 28. His brother attended him when possible; they had always been very close. The cause of death was tuberculosis. His brother Willie was a baker who worked for the Co-op. He was to die at the age of 41 in 1912. Willie's son John also worked for the Co-op as a baker. He emigrated to Canada and successfully set up his own bakery business in Arkona, Ontario, after the Great War.

### Albert Christmas 1868–1946

When he returned to football in 1893 he joined Cray Wanderers, a Kent County team, and played for two years before retiring from the game. He was later promoted to foreman at the Woolwich Arsenal. When he was in his sixties his granddaughter asked him if he could still do the splits. He obliged! He died in 1946 at the age of 78.

### Frederick Collins 1867–1937

One of Arsenal's first professional footballers. At the end of his football career he resumed his trade as a toolmaker in his native city of Birmingham. He died in 1937, aged 70.

### Gavin Crawford 1868–1955

One of the Woolwich Arsenal's first professional players. Originally he was a right wing forward, but after losing some of his pace, converted to an influential right half. He was one of the players to be sacrificed when Arsenal needed to raise funds, and was transferred to Millwall in the summer of 1898. In the 1898–9 season he missed only two Southern League matches. At the age of 30 he was transferred from Millwall to Queen's Park Rangers for a season. Eventually he went to Charlton FC, and for many years was a senior member of the ground staff. Died 1955, aged 87.

### Will Crooks 1852–1921

In 1917 Will Crooks was one of the first people to arrive at Upper

North Street School, when it was bombed in the First World War. With others he desperately scrambled in the debris to locate any living children. Eighteen children died that day. He never recovered from the trauma of the incident. Except for a short period he remained the Member of Parliament for Woolwich until he resigned in February 1921. He died in June that year, aged 69.

## David Danskin 1863–1948

On 14 November 1940, David's house was badly damaged during a heavy air raid on Coventry. He was to lose all his football memorabilia. More importantly all the family were to escape unscathed. In his later years, he still enjoyed reading the football reports, especially Arsenal's exploits. David died in 1948 aged 85.

## George Alexander Davie 1864–1923

One of Arsenal's first professional footballers. Left Arsenal FC under a cloud after a loss of earnings claim. This resulted in a court case, which Davie lost. He returned to Scotland and resumed his career as a silkscreen printer. Died 1923, aged 56.

## Thomas Graham 1868–1904

One of Arsenal's first professional footballers. On completion of his football career he returned to his home in Dumbarton. He became a dyer. On 18 August 1904 he died of tuberculosis/heart failure at the age of 36.

## James George Hill 1861–1955

Jimmy was an early Royal Arsenal player/committee man. He had useful contacts with his old club Wolverhampton Wanderers, which was sometimes able to assist with additional players. Died in Charlton, South London in 1955 aged 93.

## Richard Thomas Horsington 1866–1928

Talented player, forced to retire from football because of injuries. He became the publican at the Fountain public house. He later acquired George Weaver's mineral water company. Tragically in 1922 his son Harold was killed in action at Rawalpindi (now in Pakistan). Died 1928 aged 62 a very wealthy man, leaving an estate of over £18,000, a small fortune in those days.

### David Howat 1870–1941

One of Arsenal's first professional footballers. Transferred to Third Lanark in 1896. Later returned to Preston to take over the family drapery business. Died in 1941 aged 71.

### John Wilkinson Humble 1862–1931

Appointed as a director of the new Woolwich Arsenal FC in 1911. In the 1914–18 War as a gun inspector, he was seconded to an ordnance factory in Sheffield. While there he was occasionally sent to Norway as a consultant. His prolonged absences caused the Humbles matrimonial problems.

At the end of the Great War, Jack resumed his duties both at Dial Square and as a director of the Arsenal FC. The club was then totally dominated by Sir Henry Norris MP, an ardent freemason whose money kept the club viable. Norris's shady football deals are well recorded. In 1927 the FA took their revenge. They suspended both Sir Henry Norris and William Hall for various minor misdemeanours including charging the wages of their chauffeurs to the club. Jack was also suspended for not having discovered the improper transactions. In reality nobody at the club could control Sir Henry. Jack and Amelia continued to live at their home 72 Piedmont Road, Plumstead (where they had reared eight children, two of whom had died), until December 1931, when Jack died aged 68. Amelia died two years later.

### John William Julian 1867–1957

Played for Tottenham Hotspur from 1894–6. In 1896 he opened a sports shop in Plumstead Road, Plumstead. As a sales gimmick on Saturdays, he used to place a football on the first-floor window ledge. At 12 noon he raised the leg of a model footballer and kicked the ball into the crowd below. Not surprisingly the performances ended when the police objected. Bill later played for Dartford FC. In approximately 1906 he moved to Enfield and opened a second-hand furniture shop. While there the FA offered him a coaching post in Holland. He and his sons Joseph and Harry were over time to train M V V Maastricht, Venlo, PSV and Haarlem. He was to die in Enfield in 1957 at the age of 91.

### John Davidson McBean 1868–1954

Born McBain, but chose to use the original family name of McBean. For several years was one of Royal Ordnance's star players. Lived with his wife Annie in Crescent Road, Plumstead, for over 50 years. He retired from the Royal Arsenal gun factory as a foreman after 40 years' plus service, for which he received the long service medal. Died 1954 aged 86.

### David Durward McHardy 1870–1903

One of Arsenal's first professional footballers. When leaving Arsenal David went to various non-league sides, including Blackpool, where he was to be part of the side that was elected to the Second Division of the Football League in 1896–7. David, a short, powerful man, remained single. When his soccer career was over, like many of his predecessors he returned to his old lifestyle as an iron-moulder in his hometown of Monifieth, Forfar. On 14 September 1903 he died of pleurisy at the age of 34.

### David Edward McLaren 1867–1951

One of Arsenal's first professional footballers. When David's soccer career was over he returned to his native Dundee. He resumed his occupation as a slater. Died in 1951 aged 84.

### James William Meggs 1867–1951

Played for many local sides before and after his period with Royal Arsenal. A single man. Died 1951 aged 84.

### Alfred John Morris 1867–1942

Thought to be one of the original Dial Square football team. A local man who worked in the Woolwich Arsenal Factory until retirement. Died in 1942 aged 75.

### Henry Thomas Offer 1870–1947

Later joined Southampton St Marys in the Southern League. In January 1925 his daughter married Henry Wingham, a professional footballer with Clapton Orient FC. In July 1925 Wingham was transferred to Norwich City. While living in Southampton Henry Offer resumed his trade as a joiner. He died on the Isle of Wight in 1947 aged 77. His son-in-law Henry Wingham was then the publican at the Duke of York public house, Cowes. Offer's grandson Ashley Wingham played centre forward for Newport Isle of Wight in the 1950s.

### William Lane Parr 1857–1926

Early team manager and twelfth man (umpire). Worked at the Wool-wich Arsenal and then at Chatham Dockyard as a turner/fitter until retirement. Died in Peacehaven in 1926 aged 69.

### Andrew Pearson 1867–1923

One of Arsenal's first professional footballers . When Andrew's foot-ball career was over he returned to Dundee and resumed his occupa-tion as a factory worker. He died in 1923 aged 56.

### William Steven Stewart 1867–1937

One of Arsenal's first professional footballers. Played for Royal Ordnance then thought to have played for Everton. Died in Liverpool in 1937 aged 69.

### Elijah Watkins 1853–1938

Dial Square's Secretary/Manager. An engineer in the gun factory. He was predeceased by his wife in 1893. In his later years he lived alone. His son resided in Scotland with his Scottish-born second wife, and his daughter Kate Heckman lived abroad. He died in 1938 aged 85.

# Index